The UDL Educational Technology Guide

2020

Technology for Special Education

By John F. O'Sullivan

Note:

UDL stands for Universal Design for Learning

Table of Contents

Title Page 1
Table of Contents 2
Copyright 7
Dedication 8
About the Author 9
Defining UDL Technology 10
Introduction 16
Awards 18
Document Accessibility Awareness 20
Chapter 1 Assessment 21
    Section 1 Summative/Formative 23
    Section 2 Instant Grading 29
    Section 3 Rubric 31
Chapter 2 Executive Function 33
    Section 1 Google Executive Function 37
    Section 2 Flashcards 40
    Section 3 Homework 44
    Section 4 Calendar 47
    Section 5 All-In-One Organizers 51
    Section 6 File Access 53
    Section 7 Student Communication 56
    Section 8 Memory & Time Management 61
    Section 9 To Do List Apps 63
    Section 10 Reminders 65
    Section 11 Timers 68
    Section 12 Notes 70
        Subsection 1 iPad Notes Apps 71
        Subsection 2 Note-takers for Social Media, Web and Research 73
        Subsection 3 Google Play Notes Apps 74
        Subsection 4 Recorded Notes 76
        Subsection 5 OCR Note Taking 79
    Section 13 Graphic Organizers 83
    Section 14 Outlines 85

Section 15 Projecting/Reflecting 90
Section 16 Electronic Organization 93
    Subsection 1 OCR 95
    Subsection 2 Scan Files 100
    Subsection 3 File Transfer Support 104
    Subsection 4 Electronically Organizing
    Secondary Students 107
Chapter 3 Special Education 110
Section 1 Developmental Disabilities 113
Section 2 Speech to Text 116
Section 3 Math 121
Section 4 Text to Speech Readers 127
Section 5 PDF Readers 132
Section 6 DAISY Readers 133
Section 7 Audiobooks 135
Section 8 Google Play Audiobooks Apps 138
Section 9 Word Prediction Apps 139
Section 10 Bookshare Readers 142
Section 11 Optical Character Recognition 144
Section 12 Anti-Anxiety and Relaxation 149
Section 13 Reading Programs 152
Section 14 Reading Websites 155
Section 15 Reading iPad Apps 158
Section 16 Learning Ally 162
Section 17 Advanced Grammar & Spell-Checkers 164
Section 18 Writing Help 168
Section 19 Learn to Spell 170
Section 20 Autism Writing Guide 173
Section 21 Pen Readers/Recorder for Notes 182
Section 22 Preschool Curriculum Apps 183
Section 23 Math for Preschool and Kindergarten 187
Section 24 Behavior 190
Chapter 4 Occupational Therapy 193
Section 1 Annotations 195
Section 2 OT Exercise 198

Section 3 Practice Handwriting 201

Section 4 Typing 204

Section 5 Keyboards Apps 206

Section 6 iPad Keyboards 208

Section 7 Sensory 210

 Subsection 1 Sound 211

 Subsection 2 Food 214

 Subsection 3 Exercise 217

Chapter 5 Speech and Language Apps 218

Section 1 Autism Emotions 221

Section 2 Robots and VR/AR for Autism 222

Section 3 Social Skills Videos 224

Section 4 Social Skills Apps 226

Section 5 Early Intervention 229

Section 6 Every-Day Language for Children 231

Section 7 Learning Sounds for Young Children 233

Section 8 Apps with Free Versions 234

Section 9 SLP Assessments 236

Section 10 Articulation/Teaching Sounds 238

Section 11 Articulation Games 243

Section 12 Language Games 244

Section 13 Listening Skills 247

Section 14 Teaching Abstract Language 248

Section 15 Apraxia 251

Section 16 Interactive Grammar with iPad Apps 252

Section 17 Conversation and Sentences 254

Section 18 Vocabulary 256

Section 19 Measure Sound Volume 257

Chapter 6 Augmentative and Alternative Communication 259

Section 1 AAC - Augmentative and Alternative Communication Apps 261

Section 2 Dynavox 264

Section 3 AAC Text-Based Communication High End 266

Section 4 Accessories 267

Section 5 Low-End AAC Apps 268

Section 6 AAC Apps with Foreign Languages 271

Chapter 7 Physical Disabilities 273

Section 1 State Agencies for Disabilities 274

Section 2 Assistive Technology in Operating Systems and Browsers 275

Section 3 Mice Handheld 278

Section 4 Mice Head/Eye 280

Section 5 Physical Disability 282

Section 6 iPad Cases 284

Section 7 Switches and Other Devices 289

Chapter 8 Deaf & Hearing Impaired 293

Section 1 Deaf & Hearing Impaired 294

Section 2 Closed Captions 296

Section 3 iPad Apps Deaf & Hearing Impaired 298

Section 4 Google Play Deaf & Hearing Impaired 300

Chapter 9 Visual Impairment 302

Section 1 Visual Impairment 303

Section 2 Artificial Intelligence 305

Section 3 Braille 306

Section 4 Hardware for the Visually Impaired 307

Section 5 Take Picture Ask Question Apps 309

Section 6 GPS Apps 310

Section 7 Projecting a Computer on an iPad 312

Section 8 Document Cameras 314

Section 9 Magnifiers 316

Section 10 Calculators 320

Chapter 10 Projects 321

Section 1 Presentation 324

Section 2 Video 327

Section 3 Podcasts 330

Section 4 Green Screens 332

Section 5 Screen Recorders 336

Section 6 Hyperdocs 338

Section 7 Interactive Whiteboards 339
Section 8 Virtual Reality 342
Section 9 Publishing 350
Section 10 Curation Tools 355
Chapter 11 Chrome 357
Section 1 Text to Speech 358
Section 2 OCR 361
Section 3 Speech to Text 362
Section 4 Special Education 364
Section 5 Reading 366
Section 6 Spelling/Grammar Checkers 369
Section 7 Word Prediction 371
Section 8 Memory 373
Section 9 Assessment 374
Section 10 Notes 377
Section 11 Annotations 379
Section 12 Citations 381
Section 13 Math 382
Section 14 Organization 386
Section 15 Presentations 388
Section 16 Writing 390
Section 17 Student Communication 393
Section 18 Whiteboards 395
Section 19 Visually Impaired 396

Copyright

Dedication

I dedicate this book to all those struggling students, for the teachers and parents that help them.

About the Author

John F. O'Sullivan has written six books on educational technology, and five of those books are educational technology guides. His books include The Educational Technology Guide 2018, The UDL Educational Technology Guide 2018, UDL Technology, The Teacher's Awesome App Guide, and Teaching Projects with Computers. John has had four separate careers in education. He currently works as a Librarian and an Assistive Technology Specialist. He started his career as a Special Education Teacher. He later became a Technology Integration Specialist.

John was one of the first special needs students in the modern system of special education. As a result, he was four years behind in reading because of educational neglect. His career in education was started out of a need to improve on a system that let him down as a child and with the hope of helping others. He believes the path for success for special needs students includes technology.

Twitter: @The_app_guide

email: Jfosullivan71@gmail.com

This book was edited by John F. O'Sullivan and Winifred J. O'Sullivan.

Defining UDL Technology

UDL or universal design for learning is regular education's version of special education. You won't read that in other literature, and if you say that in graduate school, you will be told that is wrong. However, the top people in the field and the special education teachers that have been around for a long time would agree with this assertion. UDL is a regular education initiative that is the exact same thought process of how special education teacher would teach regular education.

Special education is a desegregation movement. No one is using that big word except for me. Students with disabilities were not allowed in the building until the middle 1970s. Then they were segregated for most of the day in separate classes. It has taken over forty years for special education students to get their primary education in the regular education setting.

The word segregation sounds inappropriate for someone like me to embraces. I come from money, grew up at the country club, am Caucasian, male and educated. As far as disabilities go what I have would appear mild compared to the larger disability's community. The word is the correct vocabulary. Most of the students in the self-contained special education classes that I was in the 1970s and 1980s were African-American. I would put the number at 80% to 90% in the district that I was in as a child. You cannot Google this information. There are no articles on this because there was no outrage when this happened, and no one wants to admit this mistake. The high school that I attended was ranked in the 10 and usually in the top 5 in the country by Newsweek in the late 1990s. The top rating guide was not bothered by this fact. I can't tell you what happened in every district in the country when I was eight, but I can say what I saw was not isolated. African-Americans were put into special education and should not have been. This fact is written in the history books. Conveniently, left out is how many, for low long and exactly what type of education they received. Most or almost all students that were put in special education in the early days never got out until they graduated. This makes the problem more severe, then most people understand.

If you do not know the history of the field of education, it is hard to explain why special needs students need to use technology and why it should be done in regular education. Technology gives people with disabilities independence. The term UDL technology is about the inclusion of special needs students in regular education with the independence of technology. It is about combining two very important things. It is paramount that people with disabilities succeed in regular education because we were not always welcomed there.

In my past books, I think I did not do a good enough job explaining what UDL technology is. UDL stand for universal design for learning. That can be defined as a philosophy. The problem with that is a philosophy can be defined as being black and white. You draw a line, and everything is either UDL or not UDL. Universal design for learning technology is more than that. There is no red line that cannot be crossed or a clear black and white definition.

To understand this, we have to look at the past to see how we got here. I was one of the first special education students in the modern system of special education. In the 1970s, when I was in special education, nothing resembles what you see today. There was no testing in special education or testing out. They could simply put people in special education. The idea of testing out was not fully formed yet. There were no special education programs based on populations within a public school that came later. There was one special education class for several grades. The idea of teaching the curriculum did not exist yet. Each student had an Individual Education Plan. That means everyone did something different, and that often meant worksheets. Special education students spent much of the day segregated from regular education.

Fast forward to today, and nothing of those facts are true anymore. Most special education students spend most of their day in regular education classes. Everyone is required to learn the same curriculum. Students with a disability are grouped appropriately based on age and disability. Individual Education Program means accommodations to a curriculum not lack of one. As the special education students moved from a segregated environment to the regular classes, the philosophy of how to teach them has to migrate with them. This took 40 or 50 years to get special education to where it is today.

It is hard to believe it took 20 years to get the basics of special education to work. Then in the late 1990s, I was one of the first inclusion teachers in the country. I was treated like a glorified teacher assistant and told by regular education teachers that I was not a "real teacher." My story is not isolated. It has taken 20 years to get special education students into the regular classroom.

When I say the current generation of teachers are the greatest generation of teachers ever, I am no throwing words around. What I see every day at work is nothing short of amazing. Without knowing the past, it is hard to understand just how good things are and how hard people worked to get here. That brings us to the biggest lie ever told in education, "it has always been done this way before."

Universal design for learning in the minds of many special education teachers is the regular education version of special education. For me, as someone that was an unwilling part of a forgotten desegregation movement, it is freedom. Special education teachers believe in multisensory teaching with the belief that "whatever works." Universal design for learning just articulates that in better words than "whatever works." Technology is the next level of universal design for learning for individuals with disabilities. Technology that includes people or UDL technology sounds better than special or assistive.

Yes, a number of people have no idea what UDL is. That creates confusion. There is a need to change the vocabulary to help people with disabilities. The biggest problem that I face is special needs students not wanting to use technology because it makes them different. The second biggest problem is the people that don't know the history of the field and thus do not understand why refusing to use technology is such a huge problem. I want technology to empower and include not to make people different. I spent my life fighting for this. I only wish to look forward. We do not have a technology problem; we have a problem with people understanding why technology needs to be used and to take the time to make it happen.

How do you get someone to do something that they are not able to do or at least struggle to do well? The answer is technology. If you cannot learn because you cannot read technology can help contain the problem so that it does not affect other areas. UDL technology is about opening doors for people that need help but are unlikely to be able to ask for it. Technology is the biggest change in this century of education. So much is possible with technology that is just not possible without it.

Most special education teachers would not define UDL technology in the same terms that I do. However, technology means opportunities for those in the profession. Parents see technology as a new form of hope for their children with a disability. I believe that UDL technology can bring hope, answers, and success, where there currently is enough to go around.

The term assistive technology includes a wide range of technology. The new generation of technology is mainstream and used by the masses. Word prediction is on your mobile phone. No one calls an iPhone assistive technology. Word prediction originated as assistive technology. So, are many of the other features that you have on your mobile phone. The technology is being universally used. The technology is on every operating system, and web browser. Most of the people using it do not have disabilities.

The term UDL technology is separate from assistive technology and from the term universal design for learning. The term encompasses assistive technology and universal design for learning. However, it is not perfectly defined by either. UDL technology includes items that would not perfectly fit under the term assistive technology. Universal design for learning is a philosophy that helps define UDL technology. Universal design for learning is a philosophy, and technology is a tool that can be used to work under a philosophy. However, most people that use UDL technology are not a student in a classroom trying to reach an academic goal based on the concepts of universal design for learning. Every individual that fills out a calendar does not define themselves as a student with an executive function issue. The technology is simply a mainstream tool that helps the masses. UDL Technology is about including special needs students in learning and removing barriers.

Definition: UDL Technology

Modern technology that is used to help individuals with disabilities and other challenges to function, succeed, perform tasks in various settings, especially academic settings.

Introduction

What is UDL Technology?

I choose the term UDL technology because we need a new word to describe technology for special education students and other learners with challenges. The term assistive technology is too broad of a term that means to many things and provokes the wrong image. UDL technology is modern technology that is less intrusive, and for students with a wide spectrum of learning issues. The days of a clunky device that sticks out are over, and that is why we have a new term. The term includes modern technology that is used for academic and non-academic reasons.

Definition: UDL Technology

Modern technology that is used to help individuals with disabilities and other challenges to function, succeed, perform tasks in various settings, especially academic settings.

What is Universal Design for Learning?

Universal Design for Learning is the idea that a diverse group of students can meet different standards through different means. What the students are learning is presented in many ways. This could mean, a picture, video, article, lecture, real-life examples, software, interactive website, other representation. With UDL, a student is given multiple means to express their ideas and take actions to meet classroom goals. It also should mean the implementation of

16

technology. UDL is backed with brain research. It considers how we learn with various parts of our brain. Goals should be designed for all students learning. Each student can meet the same goal or standard with a different representation that shows they have learned the standard. Teachers should represent information in different ways. I would personally define UDL as regular education version of special education. The idea of reaching all students in the regular classroom is something truly special.

To truly understand UDL I recommend that you go to CAST's website and read about UDL.
http://www.cast.org/our-work/about-udl.html
This video explains UDL in less than five minutes:
https://www.youtube.com/watch?v=bDvKnY0g6e4

With the movement of special education students getting more and more of his or her instruction in the regular classroom, UDL is a way to help regular education teachers reach everyone. It also helps teachers find ways to reach many other populations that present various challenges. The technologies that I recommend are very UDL. Universal Design for Learning might be a way to reach special needs students in the regular classroom, but it is not special education. When students with special needs are successful, they get services in regular education. The goal for special needs students is for them to get services in regular education when possible.

Awards

1. Best of Class
This award recognizes the best technology in a perpendicular category. It is the highest honor I can give.

2. Honorable Mention
This award is for technologies that are really good that people should know about. The honor can be given to a technology that is a solid runner-up to "Best of Class" award. It can also be given to a great technology that does not fit into a category.

3. Author's Pick
This is for technology that has a unique quality that has gotten the attention of the author. The technology might not be a "Best of Class" or "Honorable Mention" technology. However, the technology has a quality that stands out, and that should be highlighted. The quality might be the price or a special feature. Most of the author's picks are technology that I use and like.

4. Assessment
The award is given to technology that can give effective teacher feedback.

5. Common Core
This award is given to technology that is linked to Common Core standards.

6. Awesome Technology
This award is given to technology that the author believes a superior technology.

7. Awesome Technology Maker
This award is given to technology makers that make a number of great technologies.

8. Time Equitable
This is given to technology that is very good but does not take long to learn. You get out a lot, but you do not have to invest a lot of time.

9. Game Changer
This is technology that will change the way you teach.

10. Hidden Gem
This is technology that is not well known but is very good.

Document Accessibility Awareness

Offline files and paper files are not easily accessible. You have to be able to open a file to be able to use assistive technology or UDL Technology with it. Every browser, operating system, and device have a ton of UDL/assistive technology that can be used to better access files. This can be speech to text, text to speech, closed caption, and optical character recognition. The fact that files can be accessed online helps tremendously with executive function and supports students with receptive language deficits that need written direction. Sharing the documents with special education teachers and parents allows them to create structure and set goals for students. More parental and teacher involvement can help create a dialog about work and accountability. There are devices that can help make paper documents more accessible. They are expensive and not widely used.

The math about how many students need accessible files is simple. At least 20 percent of students are special needs students. The real number is actually higher, and that does not include students with other issues. Students that speak English as a second language also benefit from a number of online tools in order to fully access school material. Take the number of students in a public school district and multiply by .20. Private schools might possibly have lower numbers if they are not schools that cater to special needs students. However, students need to be able to access school work. Basic ethics dictates this. Many of the laws we have for disabilities are about access. Being able to access documents is something very important and something every student should have.

Chapter 1 Assessment

Assessment is one of the most important parts of a lesson. Many educators believe it is the most important part of the lesson because, without it, you cannot know if you have reached your goals. The traditional way to assess students is at the end of a unit. After you get your results, you move onto a new unit. The data is often not used to make changes within a unit. Traditionally, it was assessed to make changes for the next unit. The two units might have little in common.

Today with technology, assessment can be done in real time. Teachers should give an assessment on a regular basis to make adjustments in teaching practices. Ideally, assessment should happen during every lesson. With technology, it is possible to make a regular assessment and change teaching practices in real time.

The good news is that students like feedback. It might be hard to believe if you got back papers years ago with tons of red ink. Students like feedback in real time. The feeling people experience when feedback is private and in real time, tends to be very positive. Anyone that has used one of the many online student response systems has seen the engagement, smiles, and even laughter. It is an experience that is hard to ignore. Even the competitive nature is enjoyed by students. As educators having students competing is something, we tend not to do. In the past, it would have been seen as a negative. In this context, it works and engages students in the learning process. It's truly amazing. The experiment of using student response systems in the classroom can be replicated and quantified in any school and any subject with similar results. It should be seen as an educational fact. If you are not doing a real-time interactive assessment, you are missing out.

Formative/Summative Apps
These apps allow you to give quizzes and to do classroom assessment on the fly. Formative assessment is are more comprehensive assessment like a test. Summative assessment is less formal assessment or more basic feedback. Think of summative assessment as an assessment that was done in class to see if a concept was learned or to assessment a topic you will be teaching in class.

Grading Apps
These apps grade students work instantly. They have less of a classroom impact because they are typically used to grade tests after the fact. However, they can be used during class to give feedback on a short quiz or review. Anytime feedback is speeded up, there is an educational benefit. When teachers can spend less time on one task that gives them more time to spend on other areas of learning.

Rubrics
These are guides that give a teacher's grading criteria. Rubric apps, extension, websites, and software help teachers to better write rubrics and organize grading criteria.

Section 1 Summative/Formative

There was a time not long ago when schools would spend a good amount of money to buy student response systems, also known as clickers. The students would press buttons on what looked like a remote control or garage opener depending on the brand. Now they are websites, and/or apps. Most of the well-known student response systems are free. Many of the providers have paid options as well. Obviously, you need a device to use it. The instant feedback can be a game changer for your teaching. The instant feedback is outstanding in regard to increasing engagement. Students love instant feedback.

Web-Based Student Response Systems

Edpuzzle Honorable Mention
I really think Edpuzzle has put together an excellent product. You can show students a video or a select part of a video. You can add questions and audio-notes that can be used to explain the video at specific points of time. The product tracks progress and has due dates. You can do an assessment with the tool. This is an awesome product to flip a classroom. If you like video and are somewhat techie, I suggest you try Edpuzzle.
https://edpuzzle.com/

Kahoot Honorable Mention Time Equitable
This is a very simple and effective website that can be used to give feedback to your students. Teachers can also make changes to their teaching based on feedback from Kahoot. This is a very popular website. I highly recommend using Kahoot if you have never done so before.
Teachers:
https://getkahoot.com/
For Students:
https://kahoot.it/#/
App:
https://itunes.apple.com/us/app/kahoot-play-learning-games/id1131203560?mt=8
https://play.google.com/store/apps/details?id=no.mobitroll.kahoot.android&hl=en

Socrative Honorable Mention Awesome Technology
This is a very good free web-based student response system. The website has made many improvements. It can be used with all types of computer devices. You can use it with computers, tablets, and smartphones. Socrative is user-friendly and used by a number of educators. Socrative has apps for Chrome, iPad, Windows, and Android devices. You can also access Socrative on any device via their website.
http://www.socrative.com/
https://itunes.apple.com/us/app/socrative-student/id477618130?mt=8
https://play.google.com/store/apps/details?id=com.socrative.student&hl=en

Edulastic

There are premade questions that you can alter. The platform integrates with Google Classroom. The tool has more features than some of the other online assessment tools. That is a positive, but it makes the tool slightly more complicated. This tool is great for a slightly higher end user that wants a little bit more than what the other tools have to offer. This tool is not as well-known as some of the other tools on the market. However, the interface is very good.

https://edulastic.com/

Plickers Awesome Technology

This is a free app. Students hold up cards with their answers, and the teacher scans the room with the app using the camera of the iPad, Android tablet, or smartphone. It is a fun and simple app to use. The app is amazing. The reaction you get from students is awesome. Everyone should try this amazing product at least once.

https://plickers.com/

https://itunes.apple.com/us/app/plickers/id701184049?mt=8

https://play.google.com/store/apps/details?id=com.plickers.client.android&hl=en

Gimkit

This is not a well-known tool. Even though it is not widely used, there are some very good reviews on this product.

https://www.gimkit.com/

https://chrome.google.com/webstore/detail/refined-github/hlepfoohegkhhmjieoechaddaejaokhf?hl=en

Google Forms
With a large number of schools using Google Suite, this is a good choice. You make a form and share the link with a class.
https://www.google.com/forms/about/

Quizlet
This is the best flashcard website. Quizlet has an assessment component that is very good.
https://quizlet.com/
https://chrome.google.com/webstore/detail/quizlet/bgofflgeghkhocbociocnckocbjmomjh?hl=en

Playpostit
This is a website that allows you to make interactive videos with an assessment similar to Edpuzzle. If you are looking to make lessons with interactive videos, this might be an option.
https://learn.playposit.com/learn/

Formative
This online assessment tool is similar to Kahoot or Socrative. The tool gets good reviews. Teachers can open a free account to try this assessment tool.
https://goformative.com/

Pollanywhere
Pollanywhere has more features and tools than in years past. This assessment tool is very good.
https://www.polleverywhere.com/

Spiral

This is an online assessment tool that gets some good reviews. It not as well-known as some of the other online assessment tools. It looks like a real sleeper pick in a crowded field.

https://spiral.ac/

Otus

This app gets some high ratings and has a number of advanced features. However, it does not have the following of some of the other products in this category. If you are looking for a comprehensive product to use every day that has a number of features, this is a very good product. If you are using student response systems and you are looking for something that more features Outus should be a strong consideration.

Website: http://otus.com/

Others:

Verso

This app gets some high ratings in the app store. There are apps for Chrome, iPad, Android, and Windows.

http://versoapp.com/

Mentimeter

Mentimeter allows you to create interactive presentations with polls and feedback. The service gets some very good reviews. It is worth a look.

https://www.mentimeter.com/

Google Play Student Response Systems (Clickers) Apps

Blicker Bluetooth For Students Awesome Technology
This is a student response system with excellent ratings.
This product is just not as well known or used as some
other programs in this category.
https://play.google.com/store/apps/details?id=com.imstudio
.beacontx.transmitter&hl=e
Windows
https://www.microsoft.com/en-us/store/p/blicker-for-
student-student-response-system/9nblggh4nwt9

Section 2 Instant Grading

I know that some people think what is so "UDL about instant grading?" Using scantron type grading with an app can look like a lazy way to do assessments. I am a strong believer in instant feedback. I firmly believe that the faster you can give feedback to personalize learning for each student, the better. Self-awareness for students helps students to self-correct mistakes. You must know you do not understand the material to seek solutions. The best way to use instant grading apps is to give a practice test and grade the students in real time. I am all for lessening teachers burdens with technology. Teacher free time is used to improve other areas of instruction.

ZipGrade Game Changer Time Equitable Best of Class
This is the iPad or Android version of a Scantron machine. I know it is not a student response system. However, when students can take a test, and you can take a picture, and the tablet corrects it for you in real time, that is something special. The app is available on all or most smartphones. This app will save you so considerable time. I am not sure why everyone does not use this technology.
https://itunes.apple.com/us/app/zipgrade-grade-tests-your/id635077270?mt=8&ign-mpt=uo%3D4
Google Play
https://play.google.com/store/apps/details?id=com.zipgrade llc.android.zipgrade&hl=en
Website: https://www.zipgrade.com/

Quick Key Mobile Grading App

This app/service offers a lot. You can send quizzes to students electronically or grade paper quizzes with the app. The service also integrates with Google Suite. You can try the service/app for free. If you like what you see, then you can pay a modest fee per month.

https://get.quickkeyapp.com/

Pricing: https://get.quickkeyapp.com/products-pricing/

https://itunes.apple.com/us/app/quick-key-mobile-grading-app/id686229501?mt=8

https://play.google.com/store/apps/details?id=com.kiteknology.quickkey&hl=en

https://vimeo.com/user36865119

Exam Reader

This app is similar to the old scantron machines. You take a picture of a paper with some of the bubbles filled in. The app grades the paper. The app is free to try and has in-app purchases if you want to use the app long term. The app has versions for the iPad, Android, and Windows.

https://bebyaz.com/ExamReader

https://itunes.apple.com/us/app/id1087908283

https://play.google.com/store/apps/details?id=com.bebyaz.examreader

https://www.microsoft.com/en-us/p/exam-reader/9nblggh4pp18?rtc=1&activetab=pivot:overviewtab

GradeCam

This is a document camera that will grade your tests. GradeCam will grade the fill-in tests that look like the old Scranton sheets. They have different plans to pick from.

https://gradecam.com/?utm_source=JG&utm_medium=article&utm_campaign=freedom

Section 3 Rubric

Rubric writing is a very important aspect of the changeover to project-based learning and/or universal design for learning. Writing rubrics is one of the less interesting parts of education. Assessment practices are an important part of teaching practices. If you are going to allow students to have multiple means to meet a standard, you need a way to grade every learning opportunity that students are given. If a student can create a video, podcast, essay, artwork, PowerPoint, or some other creative process, a teacher needs a criterion for grading each. Starting out, a teacher might not want to dedicate the time to write a rubric for every new project. To start out, a teacher needs one general rubric to have a basic outline for grading.

The advantage of having open-ended projects is teachers usually get something better than you ask for. As students, we all remember a time we do great work but got a lower grade because of not following directions. As teachers, we want our students to do great work, too be inspired and to learn. Open-ended projects with a rubric that can be used for a wide range of projects are needed. If you see the upside on transitioning to open-ended projects, then you should see the need for open-ended rubrics. The time you invest will pay dividends for years to come. The good news is you can use rubrics that are already written. A teacher can also take a rubric that already exists and makes some small changes.

Rubric Maker

This website will quickly make you a general rubric for the subject that you teach. At the very least you can create a general rubric that you can make changes to. This website makes rubric writing easy. The best part is it takes a few minutes.

https://rubric-maker.com/

Rubistar4Teachers

This website makes easily customizable rubrics for just about every subject. In a few minutes, you can create a rubric based on your needs.

http://rubistar.4teachers.org/index.php

Online Rubric

This website helps you create a simple rubric. You can email students grades with a copy of the simple rubric that you created. This add on is for Google Sheets.

https://chrome.google.com/webstore/detail/online-rubric/fiiglmgmcodoglllnbfebbhkfidikfbo?hl=en-US

Quick Rubric

This website is essentially a blank rubric template. If you are good at creating rubrics and wanted to create a rubric by scratch, this website is for you. You get the structure to create a rubric. A teacher just has to fill in the blanks.

https://www.quickrubric.com/r#/create-a-rubric

Chapter 2 Executive Function

Executive function is a big word that is thrown around in special education circles all the time. We do not talk about what it truly is and the impact when someone has a weakness in this area. To understand what is at stake, we need to look at people that are successful in our education system. Many of the people that go to the best colleges, get the highest grades, have above average IQs, also have strong executive functions. We often hear that they are successful because they work harder. There is some truth in that because successful people are also able to work longer hours. The smartest people in our society often do not go to the best schools. There are many people with highly gifted IQs that do not do well in school. Certainly, there can be many reasons for success or failure. A commons problem of individuals underachieving in school is a weaker executive function.

Of course, there are many other variables that can affect school achievement. Typically, people that are higher achievers in school have strong executive functions and above average IQs. As a professional, we do not talk about how executive function is an important trait for successful people. We only talk about it when students struggle.

The good news with executive function is that it is developmental. That means that as young individuals get older executive function can improve. For some, it might take a number of years. Young students that show up late do not hand in their work, forget important details can overcome these deficits over many years. As educators, we do not usually work with fully grown adults. It is nice to know that we have the technology to help fill in the gaps in development. The best part of technology is that you can bring it with you when you leave school. The teacher that breaks everything down into small pieces stays in the building after the student graduates.

Students that have deficits in the area of executive function need technology to help them organize, prioritize, remember important details, and to get written forms of directions. With the large numbers of students with executive function issues, it is important to have all files accessible. Otherwise, special education teachers and parents cannot help with deficits in organization, directions, memory, and goal setting. Not having files online and easy to access stops basic accountability, prevents special teachers and parents to stage interventions to prevent poor academic performance. You cannot fix executive function problems with failing grades.

Sometimes what we are calling executive function issues are receptive and expressive language issues. We tend to assume that when we say something, people are listening and understand what we say. If a child does not know the directions, then they will not plan accordingly. If a child cannot ask a question, they cannot get clarification for what they do not know. Often times what we are calling executive function problems are language issues combined with executive function deficits.
Boys tend to be behind girls in the area of executive function. The same is true for language. Often times, the issues with boys not following along in class is a combination of the two problems.

Posting written directions online helps students with executive function deficits. It also helps students with language deficits. When teaching students, we have to consider students that have issues in one but more likely both areas. Not making appropriate accommodations in a classroom is a problem for many students.

Executive function deficits and language deficits are very common and significant problems. With special needs students being in regular education in large numbers, it is important for all teachers to understand and recognize both language and executive function problems. All teachers need to plan according to help work with both issues.

Yet, another issue is self-awareness. Students with significant executive function issues often lack self-awareness of their issues. This is a real problem if you are looking to help them adopt strategies to overcome this issue. Students with executive function issues understand the concept of a binder and organizing papers in a folder. Often times, students do not see the need to do so. That leads to a lack of prioritization of organization. With electronic organization, the time needed to spend organizing is significantly less, and the reward for doing is reinforced in far less time. The skills needed for electronic organization students often already have because of familiarity with a computer. When a behavior is rewarded, that can help create self-awareness over time. Lack of self-awareness, weak executive function, and language deceits can combine to create significant problems in education. The answer is electronic organization and the use of educational and assistive technology.

Offline files are not accessible. All special needs students need files to be accessible. Files that are electronic and posted online are accessible. I hear teachers giving reasons why screen time is bad or that using technology does not help students with disabilities. Refusing to use technology prevents students with disabilities from accessing files. Examples of accessing files include speech to text, text to speech, electronic organization for executive function, written directions for students with speech and language, technology for students with writing issues, language support for lower functioning issues and many other examples. When you look at the list, there are examples of technologies for everyone with a disability. Federal disability law trumps your teacher contract or past practices.

I recommend putting all documents online with a program like Google Classroom. Please take the time to look through a large number of technologies that help with executive function. Please understand the importance of using technology.

Section 1 Google Executive Function

Google Suite with Chromebooks and Chrome-boxes are becoming very popular in education. When many schools are on a platform, that means it is time to recommend programs for that platform. With so many schools using Google Suite, a large number of students that need help with executive function difficulties, this is a great place to start.

A teacher can upload class materials, post assignments, and students can upload assignments to Google Classroom. If you have ever seen a student that is having a printing problem, the stress it causes is serious. The fact that you can simply upload or share a document is valuable. To help with organization, teachers can even post reminders or tell students what materials to bring to class later in the week. You can answer questions, set due dates, and store all of your documents in one place. This is helpful for all special needs students. Students with executive function problems are definitely helped with such great organizational tools.

Google Classroom Best of Class
With Google Classroom, you can do a number of very positive things with regards to executive function. Every time you create an assignment, the date shows up on a calendar within Google Classroom. This Google Calendar can be a separate calendar on the students Google Calendar. Google Calendar and Google Classroom both have apps for smartphones. This can help a student keep track of important dates. Google Classroom stores all the documents and assignments for students. You can even ask the teacher questions. Google Classroom even has a

function to share information with parents. This access to students documents and assignments is extremely helpful for parents trying to keep students accountable. Teachers that work in the district can also get access to Google Classroom. This is helpful for special education teachers that want to help students. With file sharing, you never have to experience that moment again when the printer breaks down, and anxiety increases. Offline and paper documents are not easily accessible. I highly recommend that all documents be kept online. As educators, we want to include everyone and meet their needs.
https://classroom.google.com/

Google Keep
This is a simple note taking program. You can set reminders for yourself. The program allows you to color code your notes. The best part of Google Keep is that fact that you can import your notes into a Google Documents. This allows you to use Google Keep as a graphic organizer. Students can type their notes once and then reshape their ideas in the first draft of what they are writing.
https://keep.google.com/

Google Calendar
A student can keep multiple calendars on Google Calendar. Each class, a student, takes has a calendar associated with it. When a teacher creates an assignment, it goes onto the calendar. The Google Calendar app is easy to download onto a phone or tablet. This can make keeping track of dates easy.
https://www.google.com/calendar

Google Drive Honorable Mention

The one thing that Google does well is file sharing via Google Drive. If you ever had a printing issue, you know the stress it causes. It is very difficult to lose electronic files. You can organize all of your files into folders. Google Drive gives you the ability to share your documents for collaboration and for grade purposes. If a school keeps all of their documents on Google Drive, this can save money. Having the hardware to store documents for thousands of people and backing it up cost considerable money.
https://www.google.com/drive/

Google Slides Closed Captions

With this feature, an educator can talk, and each word that is stated is displayed on your projector. Having the visual of the presentation is excellent for reinforcement. To have a free way to display every word you say is very valuable for students with any kind of hearing impairment. It also helps students with other issues as well.
https://support.google.com/docs/answer/9109474?hl=en
Note: If the text is not big enough, I recommend using Google Documents voice typing. If you use an iPad as a microphone and project what you are saying on a whiteboard, it does the same thing as Google Slides Closed Captions. Except the type is much bigger.

Section 2 Flashcards

Flashcards are still an excellent way to help students with memory issues and those with difficulty with focusing. Both groups benefit from the use of electronic flashcards and other innovative testing and drilling methods. If you have difficulty focusing or remembering it translates to problematic executive function issues. Flashcards have slowly become better over the years. The competition in this area has improved. I still really like Quizlet. However, competitors have evolved to the point of being viable options. I have listed the best flashcard websites/apps in this section.

Quizlet Best of Class Author's Pick
This app has tons of pre-made flashcards. The app claims to have a database of 15 million flashcards. This is the best flashcard website that I have found.
https://itunes.apple.com/us/app/quizlet/id546473125?mt=8
Website: http://quizlet.com/
https://chrome.google.com/webstore/detail/quizlet/bgofflgeghkhocbociocnckocbjmomjh
https://www.microsoft.com/en-us/store/p/quizlet-mobile/9nblggh4pvqz
https://play.google.com/store/apps/details?id=com.quizlet.quizletandroid&hl=en

Flashcards by NKO — Engaging Flashcard Activities
This is a flashcard app that has a large number of ways for you to learn the information.
https://itunes.apple.com/us/app/flashcards-by-nko-engaging-flashcard-activities/id478986342?mt=8&ign-mpt=uo%3D4
https://prepgame.com/
https://nkoapps.com/accounts/login/
https://play.google.com/store/apps/details?id=com.nkoventuresllc.flashcards&hl=en_US

Brainscape - Smart Flashcard
This is a highly rated flashcard app that is free. The write-up on iTunes calls them smart flashcards. From the reviews, I would have to say they are on to something. You can also buy a number of in-app purchases.
https://www.brainscape.com/
https://itunes.apple.com/us/app/brainscape-smart-flashcards/id442415567?mt=8
https://play.google.com/store/apps/details?id=com.brainscape.mobile.portal&hl=en_US

StudyBlue
Online flashcards and study guide in a highly rated app.
https://www.studyblue.com/
https://itunes.apple.com/us/app/studyblue-online-flashcards/id323887414?mt=8&ign-mpt=uo%3D4
https://play.google.com/store/apps/details?id=com.studyblue

Cram

This is a very good flashcard website. You can also get an app for the iPad or Android tablet. You can test yourself several different ways with this app. The website also has a massive number of flashcards if you want to use what others have already done.

https://itunes.apple.com/us/app/cram.com/id734887700?mt=8&ign-mpt=uo%3D4

http://www.cram.com/

https://play.google.com/store/apps/details?id=com.studymode.cram&hl=en

Bitsboard Flashcards & Games

This is a very good flashcard app for the iPad.

https://apps.apple.com/us/app/bitsboard-flashcards-games/id516842210

Ultimate Vocabulary Builder

This is a flashcard app with a number of very high ratings.

https://apps.apple.com/us/app/ultimate-vocabulary-builder/id1262747026

Flashcards Deluxe

This program is designed to make some very nice flashcards.

https://itunes.apple.com/us/app/flashcards-deluxe/id307840670?mt=8

https://play.google.com/store/apps/details?id=com.orangeorapple.flashcards&hl=en_US

GoConqr

This website gets some great reviews.

https://www.goconqr.com/en/flashcards/

A+ FlashCards Pro
You can use this app with Quizlet, and that is a real plus.
https://itunes.apple.com/us/app/a+-flashcards-pro/id395248242?mt=8

Knowji Vocab Lite Audio Visual Vocabulary Flashcards for SAT, GRE, ACT, TOEFL, IELTS, ISEE Exam Takers
I don't normally like to rate flashcard apps that are for specific tests. However, the reviews and design of this app are just too good to be ignored.
https://itunes.apple.com/us/app/knowji-vocab-lite-audio-visual/id580351269?mt=8

Section 3 Homework

Once upon a time, special education teachers in the resource room used to check student planners. Students carried a book and were expected to write down all their assignments. Today students often have technology solutions to help keep track of assignments. Google Classroom has a calendar that lists assignments. Schools have websites and other tools to help organize assignments. With all of this helpful technology, teachers still write assignments on a whiteboard, if you can believe that. The best educational technology response to this are several homework apps. If the students have a mobile phone, the one thing I find is they always have it on them. People tend to get anxiety if they lose their phones. Once you can get the important homework data on a student's phone they will have that information on assignments with them wherever they go.

myHomework Student Planner Honorable
Mention Author's Pick
This is a very good app that allows you to keep track of all of your homework.
https://itunes.apple.com/us/app/myhomework-student-planner/id303490844?mt=8
https://myhomeworkapp.com/
Mac https://itunes.apple.com/us/app/myhomework-student-planner/id970610831?mt=12
Google
Play https://play.google.com/store/apps/details?id=com.my homeowork&hl=en
Chrome https://chrome.google.com/webstore/detail/myhom ework-student-planne/pembccdigcahnckbjcbehhcacplbbomj?hl=en

Class Timetable
This is an electronic student planner. The app gets excellent ratings.
https://itunes.apple.com/us/app/class-timetable/id425121147?mt=8

Schedule planner - Weeklie
This is a very good planner app with a number of well thought out features.
https://apps.apple.com/us/app/schedule-planner-weeklie/id916497066

The Homework App
This is a very good app that is free.
https://itunes.apple.com/us/app/the-homework-app/id561371952?mt=8

iStudiez Pro
With this app, you can keep track of all of your classes and assignments.
https://itunes.apple.com/us/app/istudiez-pro/id310636441?mt=8
Website http://istudentpro.com/ios.php

Power Planner
This website/app gets some great reviews.
https://powerplanner.net/login
https://itunes.apple.com/us/app/power-planner/id1278178608?mt=8
https://play.google.com/store/apps/details?id–com.barebon esdev.powerplanner&hl=en_US

Todait - Smart study planner
product gets good reviews.
https://www.todait.com/
https://itunes.apple.com/us/app/todait-smart-study-planner/id1083321139?mt=8
https://play.google.com/store/apps/details?id=com.autoschedule.proto&hl=en_US

Chipper: Assignment Planner
This app gets some strong reviews.
https://apps.apple.com/app/apple-store/id1437332177
https://play.google.com/store/apps/details?id=com.getchipper
https://getchipper.com/

Egenda - School Planner & Assistant
This app gets a number of good reviews and has a number of downloads.
https://play.google.com/store/apps/details?id=studios.gr8bit.schoolmanager

Student Planner - Homework Agenda & Notes
This app gets some good reviews
https://play.google.com/store/apps/details?id=com.siawo.android.planner
https://sites.google.com/view/planner-app

Section 4 Calendar

Keeping a calendar is a great way to keep track of important dates. As adults with busy lives, we must use a calendar for our work appointments. Students don't think to write down times and dates the same ways as adults. A calendar is a simple yet powerful tool. Many highly productive adults need a phone calendar to remind them about where to go and what to do. Students with executive functions defects would struggle to take the time to fill out a basic tool like a calendar. Never underestimate the power of using an electronic calendar. Imagine if we had just to remember everything. A Google calendar can easily be embedded on a website. A calendar can be shared. Several calendars can be read at the same time. As teachers, we need to take the time to use these organizational tools and encourage our students to do the same. The alternative is forgetting.

Google Calendar Best of Class
This is a very good calendar and can be shared and embed on a website. You can find apps that work with this calendar. You can use Google Calendar on a number of different platforms. So many people already have Gmail accounts, and as a result, you don't have to create a new account. You can also put an app with your calendar on your smartphone.
https://www.google.com/calendar

Android

Calendar - Agenda, Tasks, and Events
This app does a number of tasks, has great reviews, and has been downloaded a number of times.
https://play.google.com/store/apps/details?id=com.skuld.ca lendario&hl=en

DigiCal Calendar Agenda
I like how this calendar visual represents the information. The app gets good reviews and has a ton of downloads.
https://play.google.com/store/apps/details?id=com.digibites .calendar&hl=en

Calendar 2019 : Schedule Reminder, Agenda, To-Do
This app does a number of things. You can keep a calendar, to d list, and reminders for important tasks. This all in one calendar gets some very good ratings.
https://play.google.com/store/apps/details?id=free.weather. calendar.schedule.reminder.todo.agenda.note&hl=en

Calendar - Handy Calendar 2019,Reminder,ToDo
This app syncs with Google Calendar does a number of tasks and get good reviews.
https://play.google.com/store/apps/details?id=free.calendar. pro.reminder.agenda.todo.notes.alarm&hl=en

iPhone/iPad

Calendars by Readdle
This app gets great reviews and has a good visual representation of information.
https://itunes.apple.com/us/app/calendars-by-readdle/id608834326

TimeTree: Free Shared Calendar
This is a very good calendar app with a high rating.
https://itunes.apple.com/us/app/timetree-free-shared-calendar/id952578473?mt=8

Calendars 5 - Smart Calendar and Task Manager with Google Calendar Sync
This app has a good interface.
https://itunes.apple.com/us/app/calendars-5-smart-calendar/id697927927?mt=8

CalenMob - Google Calendar Client
If you like Google Calendar and want to take it with you, this app is for you. I like how this app visually organizes your calendar.
https://itunes.apple.com/us/app/calenmob-google-calendar-client/id514917848?mt=8

Planner Plus
This is a very good calendar app.
https://itunes.apple.com/us/app/planner-plus-daily-schedule/id571588936?mt=8

MyCal - Myanmar/Burmese Calendar
This calendar gets excellent reviews. You can look at dates far into the future or past with this app.
https://itunes.apple.com/us/app/mycal-myanmar-burmese-calendar/id1064604577?mt=8

Tiny Calendar
I like the design of this app. The app gets some good reviews.
https://itunes.apple.com/us/app/tiny-calendar/id514917848

Section 5 All-In-One Organizers

Google Drive with Google Suite Honorable Mention
You can organize all of your files in Google Suite with Google Drive. You can also create new documents and assign them to folders. Google Suite has several programs that are very good for organization. Google Calendar is a great way to remember dates, and Google Keep is an excellent way to take notes. I prefer using Google Keep as a graphic organizer because you can import the notes into Google Documents. Google Classroom is a great way to organize class files and assignments for students.
If your school uses Google Suite, you should use the good options that you already have.
https://www.google.com/drive/
https://gsuite.google.com/

Diigo
This is an organization and annotation tool. The website helps you keep bookmarks. You can also annotate PDFs.
https://www.diigo.com/
https://chrome.google.com/webstore/detail/diigo-web-collector-captu/pnhplgjpclknigjpccbcnmicgcieojbh?hl=en
https://play.google.com/store/apps/details?id=com.diigo.android&hl=en

TrackClass
This website helps you to keep a calendar, notes, keep track of assignments, and save important files. This is a good user-friendly organization tool.
http://trackclass.com/

Notebooks 8 - All Your Documents, Files, and Tasks
This highly rated app takes notes, organizes tasks, and documents.
https://itunes.apple.com/us/app/notebooks-8-all-your-documents/id780438662?mt=8

Section 6 File Access

One of the biggest problems is being able to access files on the go. Today schools are file sharing, and less printing is taking place. The problem is that many students do their work on private Google accounts. Often times, School Google accounts do not allow sharing outside the domain. In English, you cannot often share documents from your private account back and forth with your school account. The other issues are that sometimes students forget to bring work into school. Not being able to find documents or using the wrong platform are common problems for students with executive function deficits. Good news is that you can find websites that can convert for free from one file format to another. This is not possible if you do not have the file. A good organization practice is having your students create access to their documents on their phone. I have seen students lose electronic files that I saw them create and finish. Spending a little time getting students to create access to documents on their phones will at least give you some options.

Google Drive Honorable Mention
With so many schools using Google Suite, this is often the easiest and most user-friendly way to access files. I encourage everyone to put this app on your phone to access your files.
https://www.google.com/drive/

Chrome Remote Desktop

This Chrome extension enables you to access a computer remotely. This is very helpful when you need files from home on the go.

https://chrome.google.com/webstore/detail/chrome-remote-desktop/gbchcmhmhahfdphkhkmpfmihenigjmpp/2013/07/chromoting-nos-permitira-controlar-nuestro-escritorio-de-manera-remota-desde-android.html/null
https://play.google.com/store/apps/details?id=com.google.chromeremotedesktop&hl=en

Splashtop 2 Remote Desktop

This is a highly rated app that allows you to access all of your files. The app is very popular and has been downloaded many times.

https://itunes.apple.com/us/app/id382509315
Google
Play https://play.google.com/store/apps/details?id=com.splashtop.remote.pad.v2

File Manager

This app organizes all of your files in one place. The app gets great ratings and has been widely downloaded.

https://play.google.com/store/apps/details?id=com.asus.filemanager&hl=en_US

DropBox

This was the preferred option for iPad users at one point. It is still a good service to store and share files

https://www.dropbox.com/

OneDrive
This is Microsoft's file storage program. If your school uses Microsoft products, you can use OneDrive to store and share files.
https://onedrive.live.com/about/en-us/

FileBrowser - Access files on remote computers
This helps you to access remote files you have on your computer.
https://itunes.apple.com/us/app/filebrowser-access-files-on/id364738545?mt=8

FileExplorer
This program will allow you to access the files on your computer.
https://itunes.apple.com/us/app/fileexplorer/id499470113?mt=8

VNC Viewer - Remote Desktop
This is a popular remote access app for an Android phone.
https://play.google.com/store/apps/details?id=com.realvnc.viewer.android&hl=en

Section 7 Student Communication

Student communication is a very important part of education. Assessment is an important part of education. Before you take a formal assessment, you need to give students basic benchmarks to measure where they are. Giving students feedback is paramount to create self-awareness. Students need to know how well they have mastered the material to a degree before the test or assessment. Being able to give good directions is an important quality in education. Effective student communication allows students to ask questions and for teachers to give answers. Being able to post information in anticipation of questions is a good strategy. There are a number of student communication programs that organize and prioritize information. These are important advantages for teachers to have. As a profession, we have evolved from in the past, just writing information on the board at the end of class and hoping that everyone writes it down and remembers it. Having a record of all the work you do and communication that you have documents all the efforts you make as a teacher. I strongly recommend that you use one of the programs listed below.

Great Communication Websites/Apps for Secondary

Google Classroom Best of Class
You have to be a Google School to use this and get a full understanding of how it works. If you are not a Google school, you can use it, but without practice with students, you will not fully understand the product. This is the best product to organize student work, assignments, and in documents.
https://www.google.com/edu/products/productivity-tools/classroom/
https://itunes.apple.com/us/app/google-classroom/id924620788?mt=8&at=11lnN7
https://play.google.com/store/apps/details?id=com.google.android.apps.classroom&hl=en

Canvas
This is a good alternative to Google Classroom. You can post assignments and materials online. Students log in to see the assignments and materials. Parents get a login to keep track of their children's progress. This creates organization and structure for the students. The parental feedback from the app also creates accountability.
https://www.canvaslms.com/k-12/
Student: https://itunes.apple.com/us/app/canvas-student/id480883488?mt=8
Teacher https://itunes.apple.com/us/app/canvas-teacher/id1257834464
Parent https://itunes.apple.com/us/app/canvas-parent/id1097996698

Remind Honorable Mention

This website is free, and it allows you to communicate with all of your students without exchanging phone numbers. There is an iPad, Chrome, and Google Play app to go with this website.

https://itunes.apple.com/us/app/remind-safe-classroom-communication/id522826277?mt=8

Website

https://www.remind.com/

Google Play

https://play.google.com/store/apps/details?id=com.remind101&hl=en

Chrome

https://chrome.google.com/webstore/detail/remind/jppddpkfhdojffabldnpdacpeoefcljp?hl=en

Mac

https://itunes.apple.com/us/app/remind-safe-classroom-communication/id1059891751?mt=12

Edmondo

This website and app are a great way to communicate with your students.

https://itunes.apple.com/us/app/edmodo/id378352300?mt=8

Website https://www.edmodo.com/

Google Play

https://play.google.com/store/apps/details?id=com.fusionprojects.edmodo

Windows https://www.microsoft.com/en-us/store/apps/edmodo/9wzdncrdsmjn

Showbie

This app is a great way to share documents with students for iPads. There is also a Chrome extension that allows Google Schools to use the product as well. This is a good choice for the paperless classroom.

https://www.showbie.com/

https://itunes.apple.com/us/app/showbie/id548898085

https://chrome.google.com/webstore/detail/showbie/ojfoljd pdjoblgpbjjhjpahmkooppgjg?hl=en

Great Communication Websites/Apps for Primary Grades

Seesaw: The Learning Journal Honorable Mention

This is a portfolio website and app for iTunes, Google, and Amazon.

http://web.seesaw.me/

https://itunes.apple.com/us/app/seesaw-multimedia-journal/id930565184?ls=1&mt=8

https://play.google.com/store/apps/details?id=seesaw.shado wpuppet.co.classroom&hl=en

ClassDojo Honorable Mention

This is a very popular way for teachers to communicate with multiple parents.

https://www.classdojo.com/

https://itunes.apple.com/us/app/classdojo/id552602056?mt =8

https://play.google.com/store/apps/details?id=com.classdoj o.android&hl=en

New Guide ClassDojo : for teachers

https://play.google.com/store/apps/details?id=com.Schwec hatApps.Classdj&hl=en

Bloomz

This app allows you to share information with your students safely. This is a very highly rated app also helps teachers communicate with parents.

https://www.bloomz.net/

https://itunes.apple.com/us/app/bloomz-one-app-for-all-your/id690437499?mt=8

https://play.google.com/store/apps/details?id=net.bloomz&hl=en

Google

Gradebook

This is a gradebook and parent communication app. You can import your gradebook then use the important data when emailing parents about underperforms. The program generates comprehensive data in the form of reports. Your school might have something like this set up already. If it does not this Google Sheets add on will help you to communicate information proactively.

https://chrome.google.com/webstore/detail/gradebook-for-google-shee/gemkopljgkgplboijpanmegimckjncnc?hl=en

Flubaroo

This is a popular add-on to Google Sheets. The add-on makes grading easier and gives you several options to choose from.

http://www.flubaroo.com/

https://gsuite.google.com/marketplace/app/flubaroo/817638980086

Section 8 Memory & Time Management

Everyone has had an experience of forgetting something very important. Now think about the frustration it caused you. Imagine if you had memory issues that made this a much more common problem. With these suggestions, the amount of frustration someone might face will be reduced. That removes barriers to learning and makes someone with memory issues have less stress and more production.

SuperBetter
This app helps motivate you to perform difficult tasks. The app gets outstanding ratings and has been widely downloaded.
https://itunes.apple.com/us/app/superbetter/id536634968?mt=8

Time Manager - Daily Time Tracker
This is a simple and effective life/time management app.
https://itunes.apple.com/US/app/id989641734?mt=8

Get More Done - Life Goals Productive GTD Planner
This app helps you set goals and gets some good ratings.
https://itunes.apple.com/us/app/get-more-done-life-goals-productive-gtd-planner/id1013499439?mt=8

Productive - Habit Tracker
This app gets some good ratings.
https://itunes.apple.com/us/app/productive-habit-tracker/id983826477

Habitica: Gamify Your Tasks

This app helps you gamify your everyday tasks. The idea is so simple and brilliant that it works.

https://play.google.com/store/apps/details?id=com.habitrpg.android.habitica&hl=en

https://itunes.apple.com/us/app/habitica-gamified-task-manager/id994882113?mt=8

Section 9 To Do List Apps

A checklist is an effective strategy for getting the student to complete tasks. As technology gets more provident to do list apps and websites are one more effective tools to help with behavior. Having goals is an important aspect of focusing your effort on the right tasks. To do list apps are a simple tool to help a student stay on task.

Wunderlist – To-Do & Task List Honorable Mention
This is a very popular to-do-list app. There is also a website that you can access as well.
https://itunes.apple.com/us/app/wunderlist-to-do-task-list/id406644151?mt=8&ign-mpt=uo%3D4
Website: https://www.wunderlist.com/en/
https://play.google.com/store/apps/details?id=com.wunderkinder.wunderlistandroid&hl=en

Errands To-Do List
The app is well organized.
https://itunes.apple.com/us/app/errands-to-do-list/id318095638?mt=8
Website http://yoctoville.com/

Any.do Task & To-do List
This is a good app.
https://itunes.apple.com/us/app/any.do/id497328576?mt=8&ign-mpt=uo%3D4
Website http://www.any.do/
https://play.google.com/store/apps/details?id=com.anydo&hl=en

Todokit
This is a very highly rated to-do list and life planner.
https://itunes.apple.com/us/app/todokit-todo-list-task-manager-daily-planner/id1121126227?mt=8

Chore Pad: Chores & Rewards, Beautifully Themed
This is a simple but effect list app for younger children.
https://itunes.apple.com/us/app/chore-pad-chores-rewards-beautifully-themed/id384854237?mt=8&ign-mpt=uo%3D4

Microsoft To-Do
This is a to-do list website from Microsoft. You can sign up for free.
https://todo.microsoft.com/en-us

Remember The Milk
This is popular to do list app.
https://itunes.apple.com/us/app/remember-the-milk/id293561396?mt=8

EpicWin
This app turns to do list into a game. If you need a higher interest way to help students with executive function issues, then this is a consideration.
https://itunes.apple.com/app/id372927221
https://play.google.com/store/apps/details?id=com.supermono.epicwin

Section 10 Reminders

Creating a great structure for students is a hallmark of good veteran teachers. The structure is a goal that includes pacing, organization, and reminders. A reminder app is so simple and yet so important that it makes us wonder why more people are not using it. More potential is lost via weak executive function issue than any other controllable aspect of teaching. We cannot control what goes on in the home or the school budget. As a teacher, we cannot cure an undeveloped executive function. Within our classroom, we can create a strong structure. To teach many of these executive function skills, we have to model positive behavior. The hope is as students develop and eventually understand the importance of goals, organization, and prioritization that will do better. A reminder app is simple yet effective to help set goals, work on pacing, and remind students of what to do next. You might think this is just a reminder app that beeps. You have to look at the big picture and understand how powerful having a strong executive function is. These apps are not complicated or take a lot of time. They are all worth the effort.

iPhone/iPad

Reminder with Voice Reminders
The app lets you set reminders in a user-friendly way. The app is free but has in-app purchases if you want an add-on.
https://itunes.apple.com/us/app/reminder-with-voice-reminders/id469454389

Reminder & Countdown Pro
This is an inexpensive and highly rated reminder app. The interface is simple.
https://itunes.apple.com/us/app/reminder-countdown-pro/id515197396?mt=8&ign-mpt=uo%3D4
Website: http://www.persapps.com/

Reminder, Reminders with Voice
This app reminds you by using voice reminders. The app has in-app purchases.
https://itunes.apple.com/us/app/reminder-reminders-with-voice/id1071899483

Reminders - Beep Me
This app uses beep reminders. The app is free but has in-app purchase if you want more.
https://itunes.apple.com/us/app/reminders-beep-me/id412693531

Alarmed ~ Reminders + Timers
This app reminds you with different sounds. You can assign different sound reminders for different tasks. This lists a ton of features. If you need constant reminders, this app is a very good choice.
https://itunes.apple.com/us/app/alarmed-reminders-+-timers/id371886784?mt=8
Website: http://www.yoctoville.com/

Reminders for iPhone
You can set reminders for your iPhone.
https://support.apple.com/en-us/HT205890

Google Play

Blip Blip (hourly chime)
The app chines every hour. You can set the app to chine at various times. The app can be used to teach the concept of time and time management.
https://play.google.com/store/apps/details?id=it.nadolski.blipblip&hl=en

Hourly Talking Alarm Clock
This alarm clock alerts you every hour.
https://play.google.com/store/apps/details?id=com.comostudio.hourlyreminder&hl=en

Speaking Alarm Clock
This alarm clock talks to you and gets very good reviews.
https://play.google.com/store/apps/details?id=wan.pclock&hl=en

Section 11 Timers

Setting timers is a great way to set goals for a class or a student. When a timer is set a sense of priority is also set in a student's mind. This makes timers an effective tool to set goals and motivate students. It is also a great way to create a structure for students that need it.

Time Cubes Honorable Mention
The timer looks like a die. That is singular for dice if you did not know. Each side represents a specific amount of time. If you like giving time limit goals to students, this is a great visual.
https://datexx.com/collections/timers

Classroom Timers Honorable Mention
This is a website with a number of great timers to use as visuals. If you want to project, you're a picture of a timer on a screen; this is a great resource.
https://www.online-stopwatch.com/classroom-timers/

Time Timer
This website has a number of great timers that you can buy. If you like using timers with students and prefer a physical timer, this is a good place to look.
https://www.timetimer.com/collections/all

Interval Timer - HIIT Workouts
This is an app for an iPhone or an iPad. The app is designed for people that workout that want a timed interval. The same app would work would for a classroom timer.
https://apps.apple.com/us/app/interval-timer-hiit-workouts/id406473568

Stopwatch Timer

This is a stopwatch timer in the form of an app in the Google Play Store.

https://play.google.com/store/apps/details?id=com.hybrid.stopwatch

Section 12 Notes

Notes are an important part of the organization process. There are a number of apps to allows you to keep track of information. There are notes apps that you can type into, write with your fingers, and talk to. It is even possible to take a video or picture to save information. The idea is that you can remove barriers to learning with note-taking apps that have features that help people with organizational issues and other disabilities. There are note taking apps for people that have fine motor coordination issues. Students lacking executive function skills can be helped with note-taking and organizational apps. Students with weak organizational skills can use electronic organization to improve their ability to find papers. You can take a picture of a worksheet, turn it into a PDF then store it in the cloud. You can buy a handheld portable scanner to scan your documents then organize it into online folders. This makes it impossible to lose your homework. If you remember struggling with binders as a teen, you should be happy to know that this generation has an app for that.

Subsection 1 iPad Notes Apps

Simplenote Best of Class
This is a very good app.
http://itunes.apple.com/us/app/simplenote/id289429962?mt=8e
Website: http://simplenote.com/

Bear Honorable Mention
This is a highly rated note-taking app for the iPad, iPhone, and Mac.
iPad: https://itunes.apple.com/us/app/bear-beautiful-writing-app/id1016366447?mt=8
Mac: https://itunes.apple.com/us/app/bear-beautiful-writing-app/id1091189122?ls=1&mt=12
Website http://www.bear-writer.com/

Notes Writer Pro- Sync & Share
You can take notes with this app. That includes highlighting documents. Then you can sync your notes to the cloud services like "iCloud, Dropbox, Box, WebDAV, and Google Drive." You can export your notes into a number of common formats. This app also gets great reviews.
https://apps.apple.com/us/app/notes-writer-pro-sync-share/id1422480068

abc Notes - Checklist & Sticky Note Application
This app does a lot of different things.
https://itunes.apple.com/us/app/abc-notes-checklist-sticky/id354015291?mt=8

GoodNotes 4

This is yet another very good note-taking app.
https://itunes.apple.com/us/app/goodnotes-4-notes-pdf/id778658393?mt=8

Google Keep - notes and lists

You can take awesome notes with Google Keep, and it integrates with other Google products.
https://chrome.google.com/webstore/detail/google-keep-notes-and-lis/hmjkmjkepdijhoojdojkdfohbdgmmhki?hl=en
https://keep.google.com/
https://itunes.apple.com/us/app/google-keep-notes-and-lists/id1029207872?mt=8
https://play.google.com/store/apps/details?id=com.google.android.keep&hl=en

Subsection 2 Note-takers for Social Media, Web and Research

Livebinders
The idea is instead of using the traditional three-ring binder Livebinder does the same thing in an electronic form. You probably have seen a Livebinder on the internet. Each subject area has a tab that brings you to a different page.
http://www.livebinders.com/

iA Writer
This app is designed for modern writing. You can upload to your blog on Word Press or start that paper for school. The app gets very good ratings as well.
https://itunes.apple.com/us/app/ia-writer/id775737172?mt=8

Drafts
This app is designed for making quick notes. The ratings are outstanding.
https://itunes.apple.com/us/app/drafts-5-capture-act/id1236254471?mt=8&ign-mpt=uo%3D4

Subsection 3 Google Play Notes Apps

Wunderlist - To-do & Task List
This is a popular app to help you remember what to do.
https://play.google.com/store/apps/details?id=com.wunderk
inder.wunderlistandroid

Keep My Notes - Notepad & Memo
This app gets some great reviews.
https://play.google.com/store/apps/details?id=org.whiteglo
w.keepmynotes

Keep My Notes - Notepad & Memo
This is a very popular and highly rated note taking app.
https://play.google.com/store/apps/details?id=org.whiteglo
w.keepmynotes

Evernote
This is a popular note-taking app. You can store your notes
on this website and access them anywhere.
https://play.google.com/store/apps/details?id=com.evernote

ColorNote Notepad Notes
This is a highly rated note taking app.
https://play.google.com/store/apps/details?id=com.socialn
mobile.dictapps.notepad.color.note

Note Everything
The app allows you to take notes with voice, paint, and
text.
https://play.google.com/store/apps/details?id=de.softxperie
nce.android.noteeverything

Inkpad Notepad & To do list

This is a note-taking app that you can create a to-do list with.

https://play.google.com/store/apps/details?id=com.workpail.inkpad.notepad.notes

Subsection 4 Recorded Notes

iPad/iPhone

Super Note: Recorder, Notes, Memos. Free. Honorable Mention
The app allows you to take notes and record audio. The app is widely downloaded.
https://itunes.apple.com/us/app/super-note-recorder-notes/id484001731?mt=8

AudioNote 2 - Voice Recorder
This app gets very good reviews and has a number of features.
https://itunes.apple.com/us/app/audionote-2-voice-recorder/id1136796093?mt=12

Otter Voice Notes
This app has just about every feature that you can think of. The app boost to having artificial intelligence or AI. You can export in different formats, playback recordings, highlight text, and search for information.
https://itunes.apple.com/us/app/otter-voice-notes/id1276437113

Google Play

D Notes - Smart & Material - Notes, Lists & Photos
This app you can sync to Google Drive, app phones to your notes, and it has speech to text capability. This is a great app that has a number of features and is for someone that needs something to use on a regular basis.
https://play.google.com/store/apps/details?id=com.dvdb.bergnotes

Idea Note - Floating Note, Voice Note, Voice Memo
This is a very popular speech to text note-taking program that gets strong reviews.
https://play.google.com/store/apps/details?id=com.goyourfly.bigidea

EZ Notes - Notepad notes, voice notes, to-do note
This is a very good recorded note taking app.
https://play.google.com/store/apps/details?id=com.pristineusa.android.speechtotext

Chrome

Voice To Text Notes App
This speech to text Chrome extension gets some great reviews.
https://chrome.google.com/webstore/detail/voice-to-text-notes-app/gmhndndomhenakopchancencmdeblnda

Speechnotes - Speech To Text Notepad
This is a note-taking app that has speech to text. The app gets outstanding reviews and is very easy to use.
https://chrome.google.com/webstore/detail/speechnotes-speech-to-tex/opekipbefdbacebgkjjdgoiofdbhocok

Mac or PC

Audio Notetaker
This is a note-taking program that records your voice. This program is for a PC or Mac.
https://sonocent.com/audio-notetaker

Subsection 5 OCR Note Taking/Websites

OCR or optical character recognition is a big area of growth. Different programs are adding OCR to enhance their products. This is huge for special needs students. All students with executive function issues benefit. Special needs students that have difficulty with verbal directions are more likely to be able to understand assignments with the added benefit of written directions. OCR makes that more likely. Word prediction was assistive technology until mainstream software developers saw the need for elsewhere. Word prediction is on every smartphone made today and in many programs. I see OCR becoming standard in the future. We just have to get the teachers and schools to understand the benefits and use the product. The technology has evolved where handwritten notes can be easily turned to text. This is done with mainstream products like Google. The future is bright for OCR.

Rocketbook Honorable Mention

This is the idea that you never ever have to buy a new notebook ever again. You use the same re-usable notebook and upload the documents to whatever, online storage service you want to. Rocketbook uses OCR optical character recognition to turn handwriting into text. The process is not perfect. However, this concept is very forward thinking. Google Drive has OCR technology to convert handwriting to text. The technology is starting to spread to other software providers.

https://getrocketbook.com/

Rocketbook OCR

https://getrocketbook.com/blogs/news/searching-your-handwritten-text

https://itunes.apple.com/us/app/rocketbook-app/id1036898971?mt=8

https://play.google.com/store/apps/details?id=com.rb.rocketbook&hl=en_US

Remarkable

This is a tablet that is like writing on paper. You can write and sketch on as many virtual pieces of paper as you like. The tablet organizes all your notes. This is a good product for a student that only wants to carry one notebook. What takes this product to another level is it converts your handwriting to text. This feature is called optical character recognition. You have a buy the tablet to use the product, but the concept is interesting and useful. If you need to have your notes typed, you take a lot of notes and are willing to buy a higher-end product then this is worth a look.

https://remarkable.com/

Google Keep
This is an awesome note-taking and organization tool that integrates with the rest of Google products.
https://www.google.com/keep/
https://play.google.com/store/apps/details?id=org.ck12.app.practice
https://chrome.google.com/webstore/detail/google-keep-notes-and-lis/hmjkmjkepdijhoojdojkdfohbdgmmhki?hl=en

OneNote
Microsoft makes an excellent product for note-taking.
https://www.onenote.com/
https://itunes.apple.com/us/app/microsoft-onenote/id410395246?mt=8
https://play.google.com/store/apps/details?id=com.microsoft.office.onenote&hl=en
https://www.microsoft.com/en-us/store/p/onenote/9wzdncrfhvjl
OneNote Web Clipper
https://chrome.google.com/webstore/detail/onenote-web-clipper/gojbdfnpnhogfdgjbigejoaolejmgdhk?hl=en-US

ZOHO

This is a very good notetaking website. You can use this service on a number of different platforms.

https://www.zoho.com/notebook/?utm_source=zapier.com&utm_medium=referral&utm_campaign=zapier&utm_source=zapier.com&utm_medium=referral&utm_campaign=zapier

https://itunes.apple.com/app/apple-store/id973801089?mt=8

https://play.google.com/store/apps/details?id=com.zoho.notebook&referrer=utm_source=notebook_homepage_top&utm_medium=appbadge&utm_campaign=homepage_top

https://www.microsoft.com/en-us/p/notebook-take-notes-sync/9n1kzgdghqm3?activetab=pivot:overviewtab

Section 13 Graphic Organizers

There is a ton of online free graphic organizers that you can customize for your students. If a student types into a graphic organizer, then they can cut and paste the words into the paper. If a document is saved on a computer, it is harder to lose than actual paper. Yes, printing can always be an issue, but with file sharing and email that is easy to overcome. I recommend typing on your graphic organizers. Teachers can also customize these documents to use with a class. You can create them from scratch, but that takes a lot more time. With so many that are online and free, I suggest just downloading. PDF graphic organizers can be converted to electronic formats. Microsoft Word graphic organizers can be uploaded to Google Documents and converted. There are a number of great options to choose from.

Google Keep Author's Pick
I would recommend using Google Keep as a graphic organizer if you use Google Documents.
https://www.google.com/keep/

WriteWell Online Hidden Gem
The website is excellent. You can access a number of online templates from this website/Chrome extension. The Chrome extension has a number of templates to help organize writing and help with basic editing. This extension gets very good reviews as well. This is a hidden gem.
https://chrome.google.com/webstore/detail/writewell-online/obkdedbflcnbpillohfoghmjpekelpek?hl=en-US
https://writewellapp.com/

Graphic Organizers

Free Online Graphic Organizers PDFs
Eduplace
https://www.eduplace.com/graphicorganizer/

This over 100 pages, and it explains how to use graphic organizers.
http://www.edb.gov.hk/attachment/en/curriculum-development/kla/pshe/references-and-resources/economics/use_of_graphic_organizers.pdf

Education Oasis
http://www.educationoasis.com/printables/graphic-organizers/

Scholastic
http://www.scholastic.com/teachers/sites/default/files/asset/file/graphic_organizers.pdf

Freeology
http://freeology.com/graphicorgs/

Student Handouts
http://www.studenthandouts.com/graphic-organizers/

Edhelper
http://edhelper.com/teachers/graphic_organizers.htm

Teachervision
https://www.teachervision.com/graphic-organizers/printable/6293.html

Section 14 Outlines

Outlining is an important skill when planning writing. As a teacher that has taught writing and as a writer, I understand the power of outlining. This is the most basic way to organize and plan writing. You can always change your outline when you start your writing. The biggest mistake students make is to start writing without a plan. The goal is not to complete the work or write a predetermined amount of words. Every time a student writes, they should learn something. The goal of writing is not to make the teacher look good or get a grade. If every time a child touches a pencil and puts it to the paper, they learn just one concept, then every child would be a much better writer. In order to slow students down and to get them to think about what he or she is doing, you need to get them to write an outline.

One Note

This program wins awards and yet is not being used enough in the field of education. You can make an excellent outline with this program. There are many good features that you will find that you like. To Learn One Note, it takes time. However, Microsoft has very good free training online.
https://www.microsoft.com/en-us/education/products/onenote/default.aspx

Google Documents

You can use the outlining tool that comes with Google Documents. You can also import graphics organizers that are in Google Documents or MS Word. Often it is easier to use the products that your school already has instead of going to a different platform.
https://www.google.com/docs/about/

MS Word

MS Word has an outline feature that comes with the program. You can also find a ton of templates and graphic organizers on the web. If you are already using MS Word, then doing prewriting actives on the same platform avoids file transfer and file format issues.
https://products.office.com/en-us/student/office-in-education

Mind Mapping – MindMeister

This is a very good outlining website and app. The best part is the product integrates with Google Drive. You can also export to Microsoft Word. If you are a Google School Microsoft Word files can be uploaded and converted to Google Documents. You can sign in with a Google account. If you have a need to work on prewriting activities in detail with students that have executive function issues, this is a consideration.
https://itunes.apple.com/app/mindmeister-mind-mapping/id381073026?mt=8
https://play.google.com/store/apps/details?id=com.meisterlabs.mindmeister
https://www.mindmeister.com/?gad_campaign=US&gclid=Cj0KEQjwgeuuBRCiwpD0hP3Cg4kBEiQAHflm1gVzzgSY25ZqQi8utPBAMGfuJPro3w31fg_ZdVRDftIaAhnu8P8HAQ
Exporting to different formats:
https://support.mindmeister.com/hc/en-us/articles/218028218-Export-your-map
Pricing:
https://www.mindmeister.com/content/education

Cloud Outliner Pro
This is a highly rated outlining app. This app has several excellent features at a reasonable price. You can transfer your outline across platforms.
https://itunes.apple.com/us/app/cloud-outliner-pro/id1018143540

Inspiration Family
The outlines are very good. You could load the pictures to Google Drive and use Google OCR technology to convert the outlines to text. Inspiration makes good products.
Kidspiration Maps Lite
https://itunes.apple.com/us/app/kidspiration-maps-lite/id675831529?mt=8
http://www.inspiration.com/Inspiration

iThoughtsHD (mind-mapping)
This app has a lot of tools.
https://itunes.apple.com/us/app/ithoughts-mindmap/id866786833?mt=8

Mindomo
This online paid service allows you to create outlines.
https://www.mindomo.com/
https://gsuite.google.com/marketplace/app/mindomo/521918824624

SimpleMind Pro+ Intuitive Mind Mapping
This is a highly rated outline app.
https://itunes.apple.com/us/app/simplemind-pro+-intuitive/id378174507?mt=8

Grafio 3 - Diagrams & ideas

You can make very detailed outlines with this app. It is well thought out, and the app is highly rated.

https://itunes.apple.com/ca/app/grafio-3-diagrams-ideas/id382418196?mt=8

MindNode 5

This is an outlining app that gets solid reviews.

https://itunes.apple.com/app/mindnode-5/id1289197285?l=en&mt=12&ct=web

Suru - Organize | Outline | To-do

You can make color-coded to do lists, agendas, and schedules.

https://itunes.apple.com/US/app/id738040933?mt=8

Checkvist

This is a very good outlining website. Since it is on the web, it works across platforms. The program has a number of shortcuts to increase productivity. The products convert files into different formats. It would integrate with a number of platforms. The product is a paid service, but you can try all it for free so that you know what you are getting. If you do not mind paying a modest fee for an outlining tool, this is a very good option.

https://checkvist.com/auth/index

https://chrome.google.com/webstore/detail/checkvist/kffhfpfmcgbogjmmhcogadccojfcaofk?hl=en

Popplet

I like this app because it is also a website. You might want to consider going to the website first.

https://itunes.apple.com/us/app/popplet/id374151636?mt=8

Website: http://popplet.com/

Lucidchart

This product integrates with all the major platforms and gets excellent reviews online. It is a paid service, but they do have free accounts. You can sign up to see what it has to offer. You can sign up with your Google email. I would suggest you try it, compare it to other products and consider if you think it is worth the price.

https://www.lucidchart.com/

https://www.lucidchart.com/pages/usecase/education

Section 15 Projecting/Reflecting

I know what you are thinking projecting is not UDL. Two barriers to learning are a lack of engagement and discipline problems that comes from classroom structural issues. I have been teaching for over 20 years, and I am familiar with each type of problem. If you can project each student work wirelessly, then you can grab their attention. You ever have a case where you see a great example and want to show it to the class. In the world of one on one devices that is a problem that can be fixed. You can simply project with one of these devices. If you can hold a portable device in your hand and move around the room as you talk, that is a huge advantage. If someone is disruptive in the back, then you can talk to the class and control the projector from anywhere in the room.

Projecting with Chromebooks

Chromecast
You can project from a Chromebook wirelessly. Your students can show a project on the projector. A teacher can project from anywhere in the room.
https://store.google.com/us/product/chromecast?hl=en-US
https://store.google.com/us/product/chromecast_setup?hl=en-US

Projecting with an iPad

Apple TV
This is the most common technology that is being used to AirPlay an iPad. With Apple TV, you can project an iPad on a whiteboard or a screen. The sound will play through the speakers the computer is connected to. You can also access Netflix, YouTube, and Vimeo or play your music from iTunes. Apple TV is designed to add internet content to your TV. It can also be used to project your iPad or Macintosh Computer.
https://www.apple.com/tv/

Reflector 2 and AirParrot 2
Reflector 2 is a software that is used to project a tablet or a phone. AirParrot 2 is to mirror different types of computers.
http://www.airsquirrels.com/

AirServer
This is software to reflect your iPad on a bigger device.
http://www.airserver.com/

Mirroring360
You can use Airplay with this software to project your iPad.
http://www.mirroring360.com/

X-Mirage
This software will allow you to mirror your iPad onto a computer.
http://x-mirage.com/

Projecting with an Android

Join by joaoapps Hidden Gem
This is a unique app. You can push information from one device onto another. It is totally awesome but very different from what I have seen. You have to watch the video on the website to understand. This technology has not caught on, but it is something interesting. The reviews are very good. You could control your computer with this app from an Android tablet, iPad, or a phone. It has a number of cool features. I am not sure where this software fits in, but a creative techie could figure something out.
https://play.google.com/store/apps/details?id=com.joaomgc d.join&hl=en
Website: http://joaoapps.com/join/

Section 16 Electronic Organization

I remember going into a meeting and talking about electronic organization. People are looking at each other wondering what I was talking about, and then people started giving me strange looks. I just kept talking because I was familiar with this. For much of my career, people thought I was out there. It was not until the crazy things I said actually become true that people started to listen.

Today most schools are using Google Drive or a similar service in the quest to becoming paperless. It is so much harder to lose, and electronic files compared to paper. The days of book-bags that have loose papers, three-ringed binders, dividers, and paper planner have come and gone. You can create folders inside folders. If you do not know where you left something, you can search based on the name, when you last used the file and if it was shared with you. With file sharing, you do not have to worry about printing issues.

Google Drive (Backup and Sync) Best of Class
It seems like just about every teenager has a Gmail account. Attached the account is Google Drive and a YouTube login. If you need to transfer files to a tablet or the web, this service is a must. Google Drive is the best file transfer service because of a number of users on the platform and the excellent design of the service. File transfer is one of the big reasons that so many schools use Google products.
https://www.google.com/drive/

Dropbox

Dropbox is a website that also makes apps for various platforms. It is a must have app if you have an iPad. Dropbox links to more apps than any other service. You could use a number of other generic services out there to do the same thing. With the knowledge that Dropbox links to so many apps, it is a good idea to use this service.
https://www.dropbox.com/

OneDrive Hidden Gem

If you have a Microsoft account, there is a good chance that you have a OneDrive account attached to it. Most people don't know that you can get free email accounts from Microsoft with an online version of MS Office. That would include schools. The service is very good, but the fact people don't know about OneDrive is surprising. The free online Microsoft Office is a hidden gem. OneDrive by itself is very good.
https://onedrive.live.com/about/en-us/
https://www.google.com/drive/download/

Important Note:

For Dropbox, Google Drive and OneDrive (Backup and Sync) you can install a folder directly on your desktop. This allows you to transfer files to or from the web by just drag and dropping of files. This is very helpful if you are trying to transfer to and from a tablet. It is also helpful in distributing files to and from your students if you have shared out a folder with them.

Subsection 1 OCR

Optical character recognition or ORC used to be something that people were not aware of or thought would never go mainstream. Optical character recognition is cool technology that turns a picture of text or a PDF into plain text. Think of the power when you take a picture of a worksheet to convert it to text and then have a computer read it to you. For students with a visual impairment or a reading disability, this technology is excellent.

To my surprise, this technology still looks like it is going to go mainstream. Google Drive now has optical character recognition or OCR technology. Other platforms are starting to follow. Software developers are looking to improve on past versions of the products they sell. OCR is a technology that is being added to numerous products. At some point, this is going to be standard technology at some point.

Google OCR Honorable Mention

Google Has OCR technology to convert a picture to text. This is very important for electronic organization. You can take a picture store it on Google Drive then convert to text. OCR technology is not perfect. It can make mistakes but does works very well. Google OCR converts handwriting to text. If you have hard to read handwriting, there will be a few mistakes. However, if you have print handwriting as most young people do, then it works very well. Remember, this technology is developing and will only get better.

https://cloud.google.com/vision/docs/ocr

https://support.google.com/drive/answer/176692?co=GENI E.Platform%3DDesktop&hl=en

https://www.youtube.com/watch?v=4lApeCNK6Ic

https://business.tutsplus.com/tutorials/how-to-ocr-documents-for-free-in-google-drive--cms-20460

https://ccm.net/faq/34490-how-to-enable-ocr-in-google-drive

OneDrive OCR

OneDrive Converts PDFs to text.

https://flow.microsoft.com/en-us/galleries/public/templates/9edee2fd772845609b488a4c3e88d7d3/convert-image-pdf-files-to-text-based-pdf-files-store-in-onedrive/

OneNote Supports OCR

You can convert a picture to text with OneNote.

https://support.office.com/en-us/article/take-handwritten-notes-in-onenote-0ec88c54-05f3-4cac-b452-9ee62cebbd4c

iPad Apps

Voice Dream Scanner Honorable Mention
This app performs optical character recognition on text documents. The app is moderately priced and gets great reviews. The company that makes this app has a good reputation because it makes a number of other outstanding apps.
https://apps.apple.com/us/app/voice-dream-scanner/id1446737725

Prizmo - Scanning, OCR, and Speech
With this app, you can scan in PDFs and have them read to you. You take a picture of a document, and it reads it to you. You need good light for this to work. There is also a Macintosh version of this program. This is a great app, and it does work. However, it takes a little bit of patience to get it to work correctly.
https://itunes.apple.com/us/app/prizmo-document-scanning-ocr/id366791896?mt=8

Prizmo Go - Instant Text OCR
This is a free app that has optical character recognition for an iPhone or iPad. You can buy in-app purchases if you like the service. The app gets good ratings.
https://itunes.apple.com/us/app/prizmo-go-instant-text-ocr/id1183367390

Google Play OCR Apps

OCR is also known as Optical character recognition is an application or hardware that turns pictures into plain text. Pictures could mean an actual picture you take of a document or a PDF converted to text.

OCR Instantly Pro
You can convert a picture to text. This app can translate text into a different language.
https://play.google.com/store/apps/details?id=com.thesimplest.ocrpro&hl=en
Free
https://play.google.com/store/apps/details?id=com.thesimplest.ocr&hl=en

Text Fairy (OCR Text Scanner)
This is a good OCR app.
https://play.google.com/store/apps/details?id=com.renard.ocr&hl=en

PC Software

These programs will scan in the documents, but in some cases, you might need another program to read it. If you want to edit them in a word processing program, then you should be okay. Please read the information on the link under the product.

ABBYY FineReader
This is OCP software for the PC.
http://www.abbyy.com/finereader/

OCR Software – Readiris
This is software that does OCR scans.
http://www.irislink.com/c2-983-189/I-R-I-S----OCR-Technology-and-Document-Management-Solutions.asp

Subsection 2 Scan Files

Scanning files have a number of valuable uses. If you want to organize your documents electronically, then you have to take pictures of the important worksheet in order to keep track of in the cloud. Scanning documents is a needed skill to be able to use optical character recognition or OCR. The technology for OCR is spreading to various platforms. As technology improves, I expect to see greater use of technology. The good news with scanning technology is there are a number of options.

There are a number of very good apps in the category that work just fine. I personally use Tiny Scanner and Find Scanner. Turbo Scan has great reviews and is widely used. There are a number of other apps that get the job done. Please do not forget about using a photocopier or a hand scanner as well.

TurboScan: document scanner Honorable Mention
This is an excellent app.
https://play.google.com/store/apps/details?id=com.piksoft.turboscan
https://apps.apple.com/us/app/turboscan-quickly-scan-multipage/id342548956?ign-mpt=uo%3D2

Genius Scan+ - PDF Scanner Honorable Mention
This is a good scanner.
https://play.google.com/store/apps/details?id=com.thegrizzlylabs.geniusscan
https://apps.apple.com/us/app/genius-scan-pdf-scanner/id401818935

Tiny Scanner Author's Pick
This very possibly might be the best app to scan in a document.
https://itunes.apple.com/us/app/tiny-scanner-pdf-scanner-to/id595563753?mt=8
https://play.google.com/store/apps/details?id=com.appxy.tinyscanner

iScanner
This is a very good scanner app.
https://itunes.apple.com/us/app/iscanner-pdf-document-scanner/id1040093707?mt=8

Fine Scanner Author's Pick
This app is free and is very good.
https://itunes.apple.com/us/app/fine-scanner-scan-multipage/id534203582?mt=8

Scanner for Me + OCR
This will scan a document by taking a picture and then turn it into text.
https://www.apalon.com/scan_and_print.html?utm_source=zapier.com&utm_medium=referral&utm_campaign=zapier
https://itunes.apple.com/us/app/scan-print-document-scanner/id978697315

TextGrabber 6 – Real-Time OCR
You take a picture, and this app converts the information to text. The app can even translate it into a number of languages.
https://itunes.apple.com/us/app/textgrabber-6-real-time-ocr/id438475005?mt=8

Scanner Pro

This is a popular scanning app that also has OCR capability.

https://readdle.com/scannerpro?utm_source=zapier.com&utm_medium=referral&utm_campaign=zapier

https://itunes.apple.com/app/scanner-pro-pdf-document-scanner-app-with-ocr/id333710667?mt=8

Scanbot

This scanning app is highly rated. It can read QR codes, fax and it scans documents.

https://scanbot.io/en/index.html?utm_source=zapier.com&utm_medium=referral&utm_campaign=zapier

https://itunes.apple.com/app/apple-store/id834854351?mt=8

https://play.google.com/store/apps/details?id=net.doo.snap

CamScanner Free

This is a highly rated scanning app.

https://itunes.apple.com/us/app/camscanner-free-pdf-document/id388627783?mt=8&ign-mpt=uo%3D8

https://play.google.com/store/apps/details?id=com.intsig.camscanner&hl=en

Office Lens

This is a highly rated scanner app.

https://itunes.apple.com/us/app/office-lens/id975925059?mt=8

https://play.google.com/store/apps/details?id=com.microsoft.office.officelens&hl=en

Scanner for Me - Free PDF Scanner & Printer App
This scanning app is highly rated.
https://itunes.apple.com/US/app/id1017261655?mt=8
Scanner for Me: Scan documents
This is a very popular scanning app with very good ratings.
https://itunes.apple.com/us/app/scanner-for-me/id1017261655?mt=8
https://play.google.com/store/apps/details?id=com.apalon.scanner.app&hl=en_US

Hardware Scanner

Hand Scanner Awesome Technology
You can buy a portable scanner. The prices go from 50 dollars to 150 dollars. This is a simple and fast way to scan a lot of documents. I suggest you go to Amazon.com or CNET to look at reviews. I always recommend searching the internet for the best deals.

Other Options

Thumbnail drives or portable hard drives
If your tablet has a USB port, then you could use a portable drive to transfer documents.

Photocopier
Most photocopiers in school also have the ability to scan in documents.

Subsection 3 File Transfer Support

A limited amount of utility software makes its way to my book. Most people are transferring files via cloud services like Google Drive, Dropbox, or OneDrive. For seamless transfer of files often times, we have to consider other technologies to help with electronic file organization. In order to get people to use the many technologies that we implement, they have to be seamless, and we have to have back up plans in times when the primary option is not available. We have to consider file transfer as an important utility.

Cloud Storage

What most people are going to do in regard to file transfer is to use one of the most popular cloud storage services available.

Google Drive Honorable Mention
With most schools being Google Schools and/or having most of the secondary students having a Gmail account, Google Drive is an excellent option for transferring files. Google is so popular even in school that primary use iPads; they still often prefer Google Drive. This is just the platform of choice.
https://www.google.com/drive/

OneDrive
The school that uses Microsoft products have the option to use OneDrive for storing and transferring files.
https://onedrive.live.com/about/en-us/

Dropbox
Dropbox used to be the preferred file transfer option of iPad users. For many iPad users, Dropbox is still an excellent choice with regards to file transfer and storage.
https://www.dropbox.com/

IFTTT
This app allows you to coordinate several apps. If you wanted to save a file a certain way every time you performed an action, this app can help. It is for someone that is very geeky.
https://itunes.apple.com/us/app/if-by-ifttt/id660944635?mt=8

Jumpshare: File Sharing, Annotation, Collaboration
This app gets some great reviews. It is also a website designed for file sharing.
https://jumpshare.com/
https://itunes.apple.com/us/app/jumpshare-incredibly-fast/id1084648246?ls=1&mt=8

Convert Files

Sometimes the problem is not transferring files but converting them to another format. Often times, when you search the web, there are a number of websites that will convert files formats.

Zamzar
This website converts all sorts of files.
http://www.zamzar.com/

Aconvert
This website converts a large number of file formats. This is a very good website for file format conversion.
https://www.aconvert.com/

Subsection 4 Electronically Organizing Secondary Students

Electronic organization is a powerful tool to help students. In the past, time would be spent at the beginning of class for students to organize their school bag and binders. Today much of this can be done electronically. Documents can be organized in Google Drive or similar services. Apps that keep track of homework can be loaded on a smartphone. That is a huge advantage.

Most students at the secondary level have smartphones. I recommend if you are a Google School having students load these apps:

Google Drive Honorable Mention
We have all seen student printing problems in past years. Today file sharing can be an issue. Students should add their school and personal Google accounts to their phones. In order to see, organize, and share files, it is a good idea to have Google Drive on your phone. Students often do work on their personal Gmail accounts, and they can sometimes have difficulty handing it in as a result. If they can get access on their phones, to their school Google accounts that is beneficial. This can also help a student to download the work and add it to the school account and get access to their school work.
https://www.google.com/drive/

Google Classroom Honorable Mention

Students can quickly look up documents, check due dates, and even hand in assignments with this online program and app. All students should add this app to their phone.
https://classroom.google.com/

Google Calendar

Every time you create an assignment in Google Classroom, the due date is added to Google Calendar. Multiple Google Calendars can be displayed. Having a visual outline of important dates is an excellent way to remind students with executive function delays of the work they have to do.
https://www.google.com/drive/

Google Keep

Everyone needs to write notes on the go or set reminders. Google Keep is a great way to do this.
https://keep.google.com/

Google Mail

Students should have their school email on their phone. Time is not set aside in many schools to encourage students to add their school email to their phones. Email is a great way to communicate and sometimes share files.
https://www.google.com/gmail/

If your school does not use Google, then you should consider encouraging students to load similar apps that work with your platform.

Remind

Teenagers today like to send a text. They are not as good at email and talking on the phone. Remind is a great way to communicate with your students via text. Your students can also contact you in the same exact way. You can send reminders of due dates, tests, and updates to your students.
https://www.remind.com/

Myhomework

Students have their phones in their pockets. Myhomework is a great way to write down their homework.
https://myhomeworkapp.com/

Chapter 3 Special Education

What are the technologies that you would want to use with special needs students?

It is important to know the types of tools that you have to work with regarding UDL Technology for special education students. Once you know the basic categories, then all you have to do is pick the right technology for your situation.

Text to Speech
This technology read electronic text to you.

Speech to Text
This technology turns what you say into text.

OCR optical character recognition
This is technology that takes a picture with text on it and turns it to electronic text. OCR has similarities to text to speech. Some of the programs turn PDFs into electronic text and then read it to you. Some of the better programs can read text off of a wall or an object.

Equations Editors
You can type math problems similar to how you might use a word processor but with numbers. Many programs like Microsoft Word and Google Documents have this capability.

PDF Readers
These are text to speech readers that specialize in reading PDFs.

Daisy Readers
This is the format that is used for programs that read test to individuals with disabilities. Services like Bookshare and Learning Ally are in Daisy format. You have to use a Daisy Reader to access the text. Text in Daisy format tends to be read in a human/robotic sounding voice.

Audiobooks
This is a print book in the audio form. Often times, when you are talking about audiobooks, you are talking about higher quality recording with a professional reader. Daisy format tends to be in a robotic/human-sounding voice.

Word Prediction
This type of program suggests words when you are typing. Think of it as spell checking before you finish typing a word.

Bookshare
This is a free service for individuals that have disabilities that make it difficult to access the printed text. This typically means visual impairment and, in some cases, physical disabilities. Think of the books that Bookshare has as library books. You can get all the major titles that you would find in a book store or a library. The books are in Daisy format.

Learning Ally
This is a paid service for students with a disability that makes it difficult to access the printed text. This service is

known for having a massive library of textbooks. You can even request that they add specific titles. The collections of books and textbooks are in Daisy format.

Advanced Grammar and Spell Checkers
There are programs that are designed to find more mistakes that your average word processing program would find. They often also look for harder to find mistakes for a higher level of correcting.

Section 1 Developmental Disabilities

Students with developmental disabilities are often grouped into one or more programs at each level of schooling. Each student has potential and limitations, just like any other student in school. Using the best tools with this population is paramount. The programs that are typically used are language based and multisensory. Trying to get to every bit of potential is the best approach and attitude to take. I approach education with the highest expectations for fear of overlooking just one student's ability. When we use the best technology, we know that we are creating the best opportunity. When you can teach language with words, sound, pictures then you are targeting all learning styles.

Boardmaker Honorable Mention
This is a PC software program that is used to teach language by combining pictures and words. The software is typically used in an autism program or a life skills class. Boardmaker and Clicker 6 are competitors in a similar market.
http://www.mayer-johnson.com/boardmaker-software

Clickers 7
This is a PC software program that is used to teach language by combining pictures and words. The software is typically used in an autism program or a life skills class.
http://www.cricksoft.com/us/products/tools/clicker/home.aspx

Abilipad

This has to be one of the most interesting apps I have ever encountered. It is text to speech, customizable keyboard, and word prediction. If you have trouble spelling and talking this app would be a good fit. You can even create a keyboard exactly the way you want it.

https://itunes.apple.com/us/app/abilipad/id435865000?mt=8

News-2-You

This is a free app with some in-app purchases. This is reading with pictures to support reading. This is good for students working on basic language skills that need support.

https://apps.apple.com/us/app/news-2-you/id602677864?l=en

Clicker Sentences

This is from the same people that make Clickers 6. Clickers 6 is a software program often used for autism or life skills classes. This app teaches you how to make sentences.

https://itunes.apple.com/us/app/clicker-sentences/id575603433?mt=8

https://chrome.google.com/webstore/detail/clicker-sentences/mjjoplcogfihnioljobfdpdcfplpcnbj

Clicker Connect

This app teaches basic language for a life skills classroom or to children of younger ages. The iTunes app is sold at a fixed price. The Chrome app is a subscription.

iTunes: https://itunes.apple.com/us/app/clicker-connect/id787247539?ls=1&mt=8

Chrome: https://chrome.google.com/webstore/detail/clicker-connect/epaaaapkpeefgpmjnjmbiflgiigapoeb

Clicker Books

You take pictures and words to create books.

https://itunes.apple.com/us/app/clicker-books/id645936237?mt=8

Section 2 Speech to Text

In the old days, we had to buy a two-hundred-dollar speech to text program that was installed on one computer that could be used only in that classroom. To get the program to work, the school had to purchase a higher-end program and train the program to understand what you are saying. If you had an accent, it did not work. If you poorly pronounced words, it did not work.

Today speech to text is often free; you can use a lower-end microphone, it works if you have an accent and you can use it across settings. The advantages of technology are many.

The biggest problem today is that students do not want to be different. Everyone is different. Everyone has something they are not good at. The technology is more seamless and much less intrusive. We still can't make everyone feel good about it. All we can do is try our best.

Google Documents' Voice Typing Best of Class Hidden Gem Author's Pick Game Changer
Google Documents, also known as Google Docs, has speech to text that is free. Most humans have a Gmail account these days. Most people with disabilities and people that work with them have this great free technology already. What you should do is buy a headset with a microphone. I recommend one that connects with a USB port.
https://support.google.com/docs/answer/4492226?hl=en

Dictation (Mac) Hidden Gem

On a Mac, there is free speech to text. It is not on every operating system.

http://www.howtogeek.com/178636/use-voice-dictation-to-speak-to-your-mac/

iPad 3 and higher has Dictation (speech to text) built in. All you have to do is click on the microphone on the keyboard for it to work. The older iPad 2 does not have speech to text built in. iPad 4 and higher have a smaller charger. (The iPad 3 is not very common.) The iPad 2 has a wider charger.

To enable Dictation (speech to text) Settings > General > Keyboard > Dictation

Being able to use speech to text with a number of apps can be a real advantage for some people with a reading and/or writing disability. It can also be an advantage for a number of struggling learners.

117

Note: Speech to text (Dictation) is a function of the iPad 4 or higher. It can be used with these apps but is not caused by the app.

Window Speech Recognition
This is an absolute hidden gem. Many schools pay money for a program like this, and they already have it for free. It comes with most versions of Windows. I find it on PC computer about three-quarters of the time.
http://windows.microsoft.com/en-us/windows/set-speech-recognition#1TC=windows-7
https://support.microsoft.com/en-us/help/17208/windows-10-use-speech-recognition

Dictate
This is an add-on for Microsoft Office. With Dictate, you can talk, and it will type what you are saying. Most people do not know that Microsoft has a second speech to text program specifically for Office.
https://www.microsoft.com/en-us/garage/profiles/dictate/

Chrome

Voice To Text Notes App
This speech to text Chrome extension gets some great reviews.
https://chrome.google.com/webstore/detail/voice-to-text-notes-app/gmhndndomhenakopchancencmdeblnda

Speechnotes - Speech To Text Notepad
This is a note-taking app that has speech to text. The app gets outstanding reviews and is very easy to use.
https://chrome.google.com/webstore/detail/speechnotes-speech-to-tex/opekipbefdbacebgkjjdgoiofdbhocok

Websites

Speechnotes
Free online speech to text on a website.
https://speechnotes.co/
https://chrome.google.com/webstore/detail/speechnotes-speech-to-tex/opekipbefdbacebgkjjdgoiofdbhocok

Online Dictation
This is a free online speech to text.
https://dictation.io/

Google Play Apps

Voice notes
This is a very highly rated speech to text app.
https://play.google.com/store/apps/details?id=com.gawk.voicenotes&hl=en

Speechnotes - Speech To Text
This is a very popular and widely downloaded speech to text notetaking app.
https://play.google.com/store/apps/details?id=co.speechnotes.speechnotes&hl=en

Voice Notebook

The app does what the name says. You talk, and the app takes notes.

https://play.google.com/store/apps/details?id=com.voicenotebook.voicenotebook&hl=en

Section 3 Math

UDL technology or assistive technology for math is hard to find. There are a number of programs that you can use. The issue is once you find something for one area of math, the student usually moves on to another area of math. The number of different areas of math that can each create a unique problem to solve is many. Often recommending an online program that teaches math is a good option because it can be used with a number of different areas of mathematics.

Websites

Desmos Graphing Calculator Honorable Mention
This is a graphing calculator
This is a free graphing calculator website that is free and gets outstanding reviews.
https://www.desmos.com/calculator
https://play.google.com/store/apps/details?id=com.desmos.calculator&hl=en
https://itunes.apple.com/us/app/desmos-graphing-calculator/id653517540?mt=8
https://chrome.google.com/webstore/detail/desmos-graphing-calculato/bhdheahnajobgndecdbggfmcojekgdko?hl=en

GroGebra Honorable Mention
This is an online graphing website. If you are doing some form of graphing, this is an option. There are many tools to work with. When you create a graph and download as a picture than share via an online service.
https://www.geogebra.org/

IXL Author's Pick
This is a paid service, but it is the best online educational math service.
https://www.ixl.com/

Splashmath
This is a very good online math learning website. They also make some very good apps written for educators.
https://www.splashmath.com/

Virtual Online Graph Paper
This is online graph paper. You can zoom in and make the graph paper bigger. You type in numbers and do your math problem as normal. You can then print your work. If you are in a school that is paperless, then you can take a screenshot and save online. When you take a screenshot on a Chromebook is saves it to Google Drive. This website is simple but solves a number of problems. It forces students to line up their work and to type math problems.
http://print-graph-paper.com/virtual-graph-paper

MathLearningCenter.org
This website has a number of what they call "apps." Each of the various website programs gives excellent visuals for different areas of math. Each of the so-called apps tends to work best with the younger grades. This is a good website, and I see a lot of value here.
https://www.mathlearningcenter.org/resources/apps

MathTV
This website has a ton of math tutorial videos.
http://www.mathtv.com/

iReady

This is a program for math that is data-driven.

https://www.curriculumassociates.com/Products/i-Ready

Watch Know Learn

This website has a number of videos on various academic topics, including math.

http://www.watchknowlearn.org/Category.aspx?CategoryID=7747

Apps

Algebra Touch Best of Class Author's Pick

This app is totally awesome. It is my favorite math app.

https://itunes.apple.com/us/app/algebra-touch/id384354262?mt=8

Website: http://www.regularberry.com/

Windows https://www.microsoft.com/en-us/store/apps/algebra-touch/9wzdncrdfgsk

Socratic - Math Answers & Homework Help Honorable Mention

You simply take a picture of a math problem, and you get a step by step solution. This is an easy way to see the many steps in a math problem. This app gets outstanding reviews.

https://itunes.apple.com/app/id1014164514

https://play.google.com/store/apps/details?id=org.socratic.android

Khan Academy Honorable Mention
The Khan Academy is one of the best known educational websites on the internet. Students can learn math and a number of other subjects. The website allows for a login for teachers as well. There is a lot to like here.
https://www.khanacademy.org/
Khan Academy Kids
https://itunes.apple.com/app/apple-store/id1378467217?mt=8

ModMath Pro Awesome Technology Author's Pick
This is the full version of the outstanding math app.
https://itunes.apple.com/us/app/modmath-pro/id1111836781?mt=8
Website http://www.modmath.com/

Efofex Hidden Gem
This program helps do graphing. If you can prove that you have a math disability, then the company will give you a 10-year license to a list of programs that they offer. The application is not simple but can be an improvement for someone with visual-spatial difficulties that finds math difficult.
http://www.efofex.com/
You can get the program for free if you have a disability that significantly impacts math and science.
http://www.efofex.com/empower.php

Splash Math Apps
5th Grade Math: Splash Math Common Core Worksheets for kids [HD Full]
https://itunes.apple.com/us/app/5th-grade-math-splash-math/id504805587?mt=8

iTooch apps
This is an awesome app maker. I recommend looking at all of the apps they sell. They have apps for iPad, Android, and Windows. This link is to middle school math apps.
http://www.edupad.com/itooch/middle-school-app/

Yourteacher
This app shows how to do all sorts of math for Middle School through college in videos. It is a free app, but if you want more, it costs money. The video looks like your math teacher showing you step by step equations. They also have a website.
https://itunes.apple.com/us/app/math./id469234810?mt=8

Cymath - Math Problem Solver **Awesome Technology**
It shows you all the steps of an equation while helping you solve it. It teaches and calculates. The reviews are awesome.
https://itunes.apple.com/us/app/cymath-math-problem-solver/id1083328891?mt=8

Math Editors

EquatIO Best of Class
This is a math editor that works with the Chrome browser. You can use a free version or pay for a premium version. Texthelp has made a number of outstanding products that can be accessed with Chrome. With so few good options for people with disabilities that are related to math this app I worth consideration.
https://chrome.google.com/webstore/detail/equatio-math-made-digital/hjngolefdpdnooamgdldlkjgmdcmcjnc
Website: https://www.texthelp.com/en-gb/company/education-blog/april-2017/math-made-digital-equatio-is-here/

Equation editors

Most people do not think about using a word processing program as an equation editor. Often times, using a product that you already have is a good option.

https://www.google.com/docs/about/

Microsoft Word

https://products.office.com/en-us/word

FastFig

It is called the word processor for math. You can type many different types of math problems with this free online website. Your work is very easy to share with a teacher. The website solves the math problems for you. You can disable the feature if desired. The interface is user-friendly. You can even sign up with Google or Facebook.

https://www.fastfig.com/

TeX equation editor

If you want to insert math equations into Google Documents, this app might be for you. It turns your equation into a picture. The app gets very good ratings.

https://chrome.google.com/webstore/detail/tex-equation-editor/eggdddnmjoomglnkjhcpcnjbieiojini?hl=en

Section 4 Text to Speech Readers

The number of programs that incorporate text to speech is massive. All the major operating systems have a program to read the text. There are many plug-ins or extensions for a browser that read the text. Optical character recognition allows you to take a picture and then have the text read to you. The technology is cheap, free, or you already own it. My advice is to look for what works best for you. Please understand if you want something read to you the hardest thing is deciding between a list of good options.

Software

Microsoft Word Hidden Gem
Yes, Microsoft Word has free text to speech. The program will read anything you type. This is very helpful for editing. A number of people can do better editing if the document is read to them. You do have to go into the setting to find it. Here are the directions to enable this:
http://bdmtech.blogspot.com/2011/12/add-quick-text-to-speech-button-to.html

Mac (Text to Speech) Hidden Gem
Many Mac operating systems have text to speech. If you don't have it, then download updates to your computer.
http://www.wikihow.com/Activate-Text-to-Speech-in-Mac-OSx

Kindle Fire

A Kindle Fire will read to you with text to speech. The price is reasonable considering how much education gets lost if a child cannot read the textbook. The best part is the Kindle store on Amazon is the largest bookstore. You can download the book and read it now. As much as I have the reputation as being very much someone that likes the iPad, the Kindle Fire's text to speech cannot be ignored. I have seen the new Kindle Fire for a little as fifty dollars. You can still pay more for a nicer version.

http://www.amazon.com/Amazon-Fire-Tablet-Family/b?ie=UTF8&node=6669703011

Kindle Fire Accessibility

http://www.amazon.com/gp/feature.html?docId=10006324
81

How to turn this on.

http://www.dummies.com/how-to/content/let-your-kindle-read-to-you-with-texttospeech.html

This is a list of versions that have text to speech. What you will find is that almost all versions have it if you buy a Kindle Fire.

http://djchuang.com/2014/kindles-text-speech/

Narrator (Windows)

This will read your computer screen. It takes a little bit of time to get used to it. The program does work.

http://windows.microsoft.com/en-us/windows/hear-text-read-aloud-narrator#1TC=windows-7

ChromeVox

This is a screen reader for the Chrome browser.

http://www.chromevox.com/

https://chrome.google.com/webstore/detail/chromevox/kgej
glhpjiefppelpmljglcjbhoiplfn?hl=en

ClaroRead for PC
https://www.clarosoftware.com/portfolio/claroread/
Chrome:
https://www.clarosoftware.com/pricelist/#chrome

Speechify - Text to Audiobook Honorable Mention
You can turn text into audio with Speechify. The Chrome and iTunes app gets awesome reviews.
https://itunes.apple.com/us/app/speechify-text-to-audiobook/id1209815023?mt=8
https://chrome.google.com/webstore/detail/speechify/ljflmlehinmoeknoonhibbjpldiijjmm
https://play.google.com/store/apps/details?id=com.cliffweitzman.speechify
https://addons.mozilla.org/en-US/firefox/addon/speechify/
https://getspeechify.com/

iPad Apps

Voice4u TTS: Type / Photo to Speak in 30 Languages
With this app, you take a picture of a passage. The app translates the text and then reads it to you.
https://itunes.apple.com/us/app/voice4u-tts-type-photo-to-speak-in-30-languages/id722987396?mt=8

iPad/iPhone Accessibility

Speak selection (iPad)
On an iPad, you can go into the general settings under accessibility and choose speak selection. When words are highlighted, you can choose to have the iPad read them to you. When you are in iBooks, you can highlight the text and then click on speak. The text will then be read to you.
http://www.apple.com/accessibility/ipad/vision.html

Chrome

Read Aloud: A Text to Speech Voice Reader Honorable Mention
Read Aloud is very good at reading webpages.
https://chrome.google.com/webstore/detail/read-aloud-a-text-to-spee/hdhinadidafjejdhmfkjgnolgimiaplp

Select and Speak - Text to Speech Honorable Mention
This text to speech app works with Google Documents.
https://chrome.google.com/webstore/detail/select-and-speak-text-to/gfjopfpjmkcfgjpogepmdjmcnihfpokn

Speakit!
This is a Chrome app that reads what you highlight on your screen. I have tried it, and it works. The app works in the Chrome browser.
https://chrome.google.com/webstore/detail/speakit/pgeolalilifpodheeocdmbhehgnkkbak

ChromeVox
This Chrome app reads the words on your screen. If you want to have the website read to you, this is a good app because it works. The app works in the Chrome browser.
http://www.chromevox.com/

Google Play

AlReader
The high rating and the number of people that have downloaded this speaks for itself.
https://play.google.com/store/apps/details?id=com.neverland.alreader&hl=en

eReader Prestigio: Book Reader
This is a highly rated eBook reader with text to speech that can be turned on.
https://play.google.com/store/apps/details?id=com.prestigio.ereader&hl=en

@Voice Aloud Reader
This app reads what is on the screen of your Android.
https://play.google.com/store/apps/details?id=com.hyperionics.avar

Turn Text into Audio Files:

Zamzar
http://www.zamzar.com/convert/txt-to-mp3/
Upload a file to convert to MP3.

Fram Text to Speech
http://www.fromtexttospeech.com/
Cut and paste text to create an audio file.

Section 5 PDF Readers

Adobe Reader
Most people do not know that this program will read the text to you. It is free, awesome, and most if not all PCs have this program.
https://helpx.adobe.com/reader/11/using/accessibility-features.html

Texthelp PDF Reader
This app will read and annotate PDFs. The app is often used with Read & Write from Texthelp.
https://chrome.google.com/webstore/detail/texthelp-pdf-reader/feepmdlmhplaojabeoecaobfmibooaid?hl=en-GB

PDF Voice Reader Pro
This app reads PDFs for you. You can even read the text in 30 different languages. Best of all, the apps integrate with a number of online storages services, including Google Drive.
https://itunes.apple.com/us/app/pdf-voice-reader-pro/id1227429378?mt=8

ClaroPDF - Accessible Pro PDF Reader and Viewer with text to speech (TTS) and annotations
This app allows you to annotate a PDF, and then it reads it to you.
https://itunes.apple.com/us/app/claropdf-accessible-pro-pdf/id633997623?mt=8

Section 6 DAISY Readers

DAISY format is designed for people with disabilities. You have to qualify for services like Bookshare and Learning Ally in order to use a DAISY reader. In the past, people used to buy expensive readers for services like this. Today you can get an app on a tablet or a smartphone to do the same thing. There are also websites and extensions that do the same thing.

Voice Dream Reader Best of Class for an iPad
Dream Voice Reader can be used with a Bookshare membership to read DAISY format.
https://itunes.apple.com/us/app/voice-dream-reader-text-to/id496177674?mt=8
Google   Play
https://play.google.com/store/apps/details?id=voicedream.reader

Bookshare
A free service for talking books for people that qualify based on disability.
https://www.bookshare.org/cms
https://chrome.google.com/webstore/detail/bookshare-web-reader/bkfmjmjngglphchhiemnghidpnddofmo?hl=en-US

Learning Ally Link

This is a DAISY reader for Ally Learning.

https://itunes.apple.com/us/app/learning-ally-link/id906070888?mt=12

https://chrome.google.com/webstore/detail/learning-ally-link/gdicnpbaekbefjanokchpfhnaphfnphl?hl=en-US

Website: https://www.learningally.org

Mac https://itunes.apple.com/us/app/learning-ally-link/id906070888?mt=12

Learning Ally has software that will work with a computer. You have to be a member to download it.

https://go.learningally.org/college-adults/adults-take-the-tour/adults-features-players/

Learning Ally Google Play

https://play.google.com/store/apps/details?id=org.learninga lly.LinkMobile&hl=en

Dolphin EasyReader

This app is free and user-friendly. EasyReader is a good app for younger students. It highlights what it reads to you as well, and that is a plus.

https://itunes.apple.com/us/app/dolphin-easyreader/id1161662515?mt=8

https://play.google.com/store/apps/details?id=com.yourdol phin.easyreader&hl=en_US

https://yourdolphin.com/products/education/easyreader-for-windows

Section 7 Audiobooks

Once you figure out that you can have everything read to you for free on all platforms, then you find a new problem. Students complain that the voice is robotic, and that makes it hard to focus. The options on audiobooks have increased in recent years. There are free services to pick from and a number of paid services that have large libraries of audiobooks. This can be helpful for the visually impaired, students that have reading disabilities and attentional problems. When you find audiobooks that meet a need, this can relieve stress and get the student to focus on the work again.

OverDrive Author's Pick
Most public libraries with eBooks have OverDrive. You can download some movies and audiobooks with this service. Once you log on the app for one library, you can also download material from other libraries, that you are eligible to take out books or audiobooks from.
https://www.overdrive.com/
https://gsuite.google.com/marketplace/app/overdrive/25415
8829526
https://chrome.google.com/webstore/detail/overdrive/fnhgf
occpcjdnjcobejogdnlnidceemb?hl=en

Libby, by OverDrive

This app is used to access OverDrive. The rating on this app is outstanding. If you plan like to use high-quality audiobooks, this app is a great option for accessing OverDrive.

https://apps.apple.com/us/app/libby-by-overdrive/id1076402606

https://play.google.com/store/apps/details?id=com.overdrive.mobile.android.libby&hl=en_US

Audible

You have to pay a fee, but you get access to a number of books high-quality recordings.

http://www.audible.com/

https://itunes.apple.com/us/app/audible-audio-books-original-series-podcasts/id379693831?mt=8

https://play.google.com/store/apps/details?id=com.audible.application&hl=en

YouTube

You can find a ton of free audiobooks on YouTube. The only problem is that many of the audiobooks are under copyright. I would recommend buying the resources that you need. If a student has a disability, even a temporary disability, services like Bookshare will give you the materials for free.

https://www.youtube.com/

LibriVox Audio Books
This has a ton of free audiobooks. The app claims to have 24,000 audiobooks. You can also pay for a pro version of the app. The free version's app ratings are awesome.
https://itunes.apple.com/us/app/librivox-audio-books/id596159212?mt=8
Pro Version:
https://itunes.apple.com/us/app/librivox-audio-books-pro/id662558935?mt=8
https://librivox.org/

Gutenberg Reader
This app has a speech to text and thousands of free books. You can bookmark multiple books. The app even enlarges text. This app gets outstanding reviews.
https://itunes.apple.com/us/app/gutenberg-reader/id1294103623

Audiobooks
This app has thousands of free recorded books. You can even buy a few more. The app is also highly rated.
https://itunes.apple.com/us/app/audiobooks/id311507490?mt=8

Audiobooks 7K+ - High-Quality Audio Books Library
This app has thousands of free audiobooks. You can pay to remove ads if you want. The app gets some good ratings.
https://itunes.apple.com/us/app/audiobooks-7k-high-quality-audio-books-library/id737369671?mt=8

Section 8 Google Play Audiobooks Apps

Audible for Android
This is a popular app for people that want to use audiobooks.
https://play.google.com/store/apps/details?id=com.audible.application
Website: http://www.audible.com/
https://itunes.apple.com/us/app/audiobooks-from-audible/id379693831?mt=8

Smart AudioBook Player
This app gets a good rating.
https://play.google.com/store/apps/details?id=ak.alizandro.smartaudiobookplayer

LibriVox Audio Books Free
This app has a ton of free audiobooks.
https://play.google.com/store/apps/details?id=app.librivox.android&hl=en_US

Section 9 Word Prediction Apps

Word prediction is one of the best ways to help a student with writing. It helps students insert a correctly spelled word that they otherwise might misspell. The student also has to use fewer keystrokes to type the same information. Word prediction is an area that is often used to help students with a number of issues. These might include spelling, fine motor coordination, or other writing issues. Word prediction can help remove a number of barriers to learning. Word prediction is starting to appear on more and more apps. Word Prediction is excellent for anyone with writing issues.

Read & Write (Chrome Extension) Best of Class
This Chrome extension has just about everything. Read & Write has word prediction that is excellent. The app has a picture dictionary. The extension has speech to text and text to speech. The app creates a floating toolbar in the Chrome browser. This means a student can use Read & Write across all settings. It also means that a student can use Read & Write on any computer. That can eliminate the need for a laptop to travel with the student. It also means that a student could use this product at home with no extra cost or risk on the part of the school. The subscription is priced on the number of licenses purchased. The more licenses purchased, the less per license.
https://chrome.google.com/webstore/detail/readwrite-for-google-chro/inoeonmfapjbbkmdafoankkfajkcphgd
A teacher can get this extension for free. This allows teachers to test out the product.
https://www.texthelp.com/en-us/products/read-write/free-for-teachers/

Voice Dream Writer Honorable Mention

This is a very good word prediction app. The app will type what you say. All you do is click on the microphone on the keyboard. It also makes some basic corrections. The app will even read back what you typed. This is an awesome app.

https://itunes.apple.com/us/app/voice-dream-writer/id920583100?mt=8

Website http://www.voicedream.com/writer/

Word Q US 1 (Chrome)

This is a very good word prediction app.

https://chrome.google.com/webstore/detail/wordq-us-i/pojcommghdpcglmnodkpcdiknjfcgoge

WordQ CA II

This is the Canadian version of the extension.

https://chrome.google.com/webstore/detail/wordq-ca-ii/ceifggnbcfkadampobhopkafjgfcfaac?hl=en

Co:Writer Universal (Extension)

This is a word prediction program.

https://chrome.google.com/webstore/detail/cowriter-universal-extens/ifajfiofeifbbhbionejdliodenmecna?hl=en

iWord Q

This is a word prediction software app. It is similar to Word Q for the PC. The app will not read web pages and does not work with Speak Q like the full PC program. The app makes suggestions of the correct spelling of what you are trying to type and then will read the words back to you.

https://itunes.apple.com/us/app/iwordq-us/id557929840?mt=8

Clickers Docs

This is a simple word processor with a word prediction program. The people that created Clickers 6 made this app. https://itunes.apple.com/us/app/clicker-docs/id575608215?mt=8

Read&Write for iPad

The app has a spell checker, word prediction, dictionary, text to speech, and a picture dictionary. The app can also import and share a document. https://itunes.apple.com/us/app/read-write-for-ipad/id934749270

Typ-O HD

This is a good word prediction app. https://itunes.apple.com/us/app/typ-o-hd-writing-is-for-everybody!/id372971659?mt=8

Section 10 Bookshare Readers

Voice Dream Reader Honorable Mention
This is the best app for Daisy readers and Bookshare.
https://itunes.apple.com/us/app/voice-dream-reader/id496177674?mt=8
https://play.google.com/store/apps/details?id=voicedream.reader&hl=en
http://www.voicedream.com/

Dolphin EasyReader Honorable Mention
This app is free and has a simple interface. The interface makes use by younger students easier.
https://itunes.apple.com/us/app/dolphin-easyreader/id1161662515?mt=8

Bookshare Web Reader Honorable Mention
This reads Bookshare books with your Chrome browser.
https://chrome.google.com/webstore/detail/bookshare-web-reader/bkfmjmjngglphchhiemnghidpnddofmo

Bookshare
This gives you all the readers that Bookshare recommends.
https://www.bookshare.org/cms/member-preferred-tools

Capti Voice Narrator

According to the write up on the iTunes store, "You can listen to any content from Safari, Chrome, Google Drive, Dropbox, Bookshare, or Gutenberg." It is free to download. However, there are a number of in-app purchases.

https://itunes.apple.com/us/app/capti-voice-narrator/id437052502?mt=8

The PC version:

https://www.captivoice.com/capti-site/public/entry/download

About Capti Voice Narrator

https://www.captivoice.com/capti-site/public/entry/about_us

Chrome:

https://chrome.google.com/webstore/detail/capti-voice/nlngjmhlfdekmgoaaiendhkcbhdcedjh

Open Lore

This is a PC program that allows you to access Bookshare.

http://www.open-lore.com/products/open-lore-read-bookshare-edition?channel=buy_button&referer=http%3A//www.open-lore.com/pages/bookshare-edition-test-page&variant=4922120385

Open Lore Full Version

This software reads eBooks and electronic texts.

http://www.open-lore.com/products/read?channel=buy_button&referer=https%3A%2F%2F%2Ftest&variant=392766698

Section 11 Optical Character Recognition

OCR is also known as optical character recognition, is an application or hardware that turns pictures into plain text. Pictures could mean an actual picture you take or a PDF converted to text. You can find applications that read the text in this book. You can also look at the section on text to speech readers. OCR software can scan in text and in some cases read it to you.

Seeing AI: Talking Camera for the Blind Honorable Mention
This free app gives someone with low vision information about their surroundings. The app also reads text to you. The app gets excellent reviews.
https://itunes.apple.com/us/app/seeing-ai-talking-camera-for-the-blind/id999062298?mt=8
https://www.microsoft.com/en-us/seeing-ai/

Voice Dream Scanner Honorable Mention
This is a highly rated optical character recognition scanner. You can take a picture of text and then have the app read it to you. You can then save the text and export into different formats.
https://itunes.apple.com/us/app/voice-dream-scanner/id1446737725?mt=8&ign-mpt=uo%3D8
https://play.google.com/store/apps/details?id=voicedream.reader&hl=en_US

Microsoft Office Lens|PDF Scan

This app is a scanner that also converts pictures to text. The reviews are also good. This product can be used to import reading material into OneNote.

https://itunes.apple.com/us/app/microsoft-office-lens-pdf-scan/id975925059?mt=8

https://play.google.com/store/apps/details?id=com.microsoft.office.officelens&hl=en_US

https://support.office.com/en-us/article/what-is-office-lens-f5f6b88d-356f-4037-b7e8-49f34be86db3

Claro ScanPen

With this app, you take a picture of a document. It will read the part of the document that you choose. You can even annotate the document.

https://itunes.apple.com/us/app/claro-scanpen/id994933713?mt=8

Claro ScanPen Premium

https://itunes.apple.com/us/app/claro-scanpen-premium/id1261399270

Prizmo - Scanning, OCR, and Speech

With this app, you can scan in PDFs and have them read to you. You take a picture of a document and it reads it to you. You need good light for this to work. There is also a Macintosh version of this program. This is a great app, and it does work. However, it takes a little bit of patience to get it to work correctly.

https://itunes.apple.com/us/app/prizmo-document-scanning-ocr/id366791896?mt=8

knfbReader

This app is the most highly rated in this category. The price is higher than some might expect for an app. I see OCR text readers as a big market for people with reading disabilities, visual impairments and other disabilities that affect your ability to read. Often times the cost of not using cutting edge technology is much higher for people with disabilities. This app can change lives and is well worth it for the right buyer.

https://itunes.apple.com/us/app/knfb-reader/id849732663?mt=8

https://play.google.com/store/apps/details?id=com.sensotec.knfbreader&hl=en

https://www.microsoft.com/en-us/store/p/knfb-reader/9nblggh6hqkk

SeeNSpeak

This app can read text to you and translate into different languages. You can also buy in-app purchases.

https://apps.apple.com/us/app/seenspeak/id1217183447

Augmenta11y

This app is designed for someone that is dyslexic to be able to read everyday items. The idea is that if you have a child with a reading disability activity reading, with help, everyday instances that will improve reading skills. The natural positive consequences of reading everyday items help improve reading skills. The idea is sound. However, this type of app is typically used with individuals with visual impairments. I like the concept because it shows an understanding of how people learn to read.

https://itunes.apple.com/in/app/augmenta11y/id1455001449?mt=8&ref=oswaldlabs.com&utm_source=oswald_labs&utm_medium=website&utm_campaign=external_link&utm_content=oswaldlabs.com

https://play.google.com/store/apps/category/GAME

Prizmo Go - Instant Text OCR
This app gets good reviews. The app includes in-app purchases.
https://itunes.apple.com/us/app/prizmo-go-instant-text-ocr/id1183367390

Google Play OCR Apps

OCR also is known as Optical character recognition, is an application or hardware that turns pictures into plain text. Pictures could mean an actual picture you take of a document or a PDF converted to text.

OCR Instantly Pro
You can convert a picture to text. This app can translate text into a different language.
https://play.google.com/store/apps/details?id=com.thesimplest.ocrpro&hl=en
Free
https://play.google.com/store/apps/details?id=com.thesimplest.ocr&hl=en

Text Fairy (OCR Text Scanner)
This is a good OCR app.
https://play.google.com/store/apps/details?id=com.renard.ocr&hl=en

PC Software

These programs will scan in the documents but in some cases, you might need another program to read it. If you want to edit them in a word processing program, then you should be okay. Please read the information on the link under the product.

ABBYY FineReader
This is OCP software for the PC.
http://www.abbyy.com/finereader/

OCR Software – Readiris
This is software that does OCR scans.
http://www.irislink.com/c2-983-189/I-R-I-S----OCR-Technology-and-Document-Management-Solutions.aspx

Section 12 Anti-Anxiety and Relaxation

People don't think about anxiety being helped with technology. Often times we think about technology when it does not work and actually creates anxiety. There are a ton of self-hypnosis videos on YouTube and a number of apps. In a world where drugs are often subscribed, it is always good to have other alternatives. I am not saying someone shouldn't consider drugs. Basic things like exercise, positive thinking and self-hypnosis can make a hard situation better. I have used self-hypnosis. It is not easy to convince people to use self-hypnosis. What I can tell you is that if you are stressed about a bad day, it can change your state of mind. It is a great way to relax your muscles before bed.

Calm
This is a very popular relaxation app that gets outstanding reviews.
https://apps.apple.com/us/app/calm/id571800810

Headspace
This app teaches you how to meditate.
https://itunes.apple.com/us/app/headspace-meditation-techniques/id493145008?mt=8&ign-mpt=uo%3D4

YouTube
YouTube has a ton of self-hypnosis videos. I suggest that you look for some videos that meet your needs. There are too many diverse videos to endorse. Everyone has different tastes and interests. The good news is there is a lot to choose from.
https://www.youtube.com/

Relax Melodies Premium HD: Sleep Zen sounds & white noise for meditation, yoga and baby relaxation
I think stress reduction is an important aspect of being successful. I like this app to help fall asleep.
https://itunes.apple.com/us/app/relax-melodies-premium-hd/id364909179?mt=8&ign-mpt=uo%3D4

Relax Melodies: Sleep Sounds
This app helps you relax before you go to sleep.
https://apps.apple.com/us/app/relax-melodies-sleep-sounds/id314498713

Mindbliss: Meditate Calm, Relax & Sleep Well
This is a highly rated app that will help you relax.
https://itunes.apple.com/app/apple-store/id1092634583?mt=8

Pacifica - Anxiety, Stress, & Depression relief
This is a popular highly rated anti-anxiety app. The app has also won a number of accolades.
https://itunes.apple.com/us/app/pacifica-anxiety-stress-depression-relief/id922968861?mt=8&ign-mpt=uo%3D4

Relax Meditation: Guided Mind
This app helps you meditate.
https://apps.apple.com/us/app/relax-meditation-guided-mind/id367506176

Stop, Breathe & Think
This app teaches you how to meditate.
https://itunes.apple.com/us/app/stop-breathe-think/id778848692?mt=8

Brain Wave

This app allows you to listen to sounds to help you focus on a specific state of mind.

https://itunes.apple.com/us/app/brain-wave-30-advanced-binaural/id307219387?mt=8

Website: http://www.banzailabs.com/

Ipnos Soft

This company has a number of highly rated relation apps.

http://www.ipnossoft.com/apps/

Section 13 Reading Programs

These are some inexpensive ways to help teach reading skills to students of all ages. Finding good materials for students to use can make a real difference. Teachers are busy, and making material is time-consuming. If you can add good material to what you do in the classroom, that is a big positive.

Subscription
Reading Programs
These are programs that have a subscription or have a paid option.

Immersive Reader (OneNote Learning Tools)
This is one of the best-hidden gems ever. OneNote Learning Tools has many totally awesome features. If you open a document in OneNote, there is a list of amazing things you can do. You can color code the grammar. The program to read to you and blackout distractions. If you have access to OneNote check these amazing features out. Note: There are some instances where Microsoft products are free for students and or schools.
Video: https://www.youtube.com/watch?time_continue=234&v=Ca_1iDuV3Z0
https://support.office.com/en-us/article/use-immersive-reader-for-onenote-10712138-b4ed-4513-958d-d9a1b3038170

Fluency Tutor

This product tracks students as they read out loud in school or at home. Students read web content or Google Documents. A text to speech feature can read the document to them and highlight each word. The student can then read and record their voice for the teacher. Imagine having students do reading at home, track each student progress, give student feedback and having the technology to support struggling readers. This is a good product to work on reading Fluency.

https://www.texthelp.com/en-us/products/fluencytutor.aspx

Actively Learn

This is a popular reading program that gives personalized instruction. The rates are also very good.

https://www.activelylearn.com/

Read Live

This is a reading fluency program.

https://www.readnaturally.com/product/read-naturally-live
https://itunes.apple.com/us/app/read-naturally-live/id821028327?mt=8

Kids A-Z

This is a leveled reading program that uses an app as a gateway to the program.

iTunes: https://itunes.apple.com/us/app/kids-a-z/id474207297?mt=8

Google
Play: https://play.google.com/store/apps/details?id=com.learninga_z.onyourown&hl=en

Chrome: https://chrome.google.com/webstore/detail/kids-a-z/pifccnhncmnilgbnnkjkgicpkeclodpd?hl=en-US

Lexia Reading Core5
This app/reading program teaches core language.
https://itunes.apple.com/us/app/lexia-reading-core5/id623853404?mt=8
Chrome: https://chrome.google.com/webstore/detail/lexia-reading-core5/jiaoahhgjennidohjjhdcfefikghgple?hl=en

Lexia
This is an intervention program that is for struggling readers that target specific areas.
http://www.lexialearning.com/

Orton-Gillingham
The well-known phonics program has an online version.
http://www.ortongillinghamonlinetutor.com/

LeVar Burton Kids Skybrary
This website has a number of opportunities for reading for younger students. This product can be used with an individual student, small groups, or entire classes. The website gets good reviews.
https://www.levarburtonkids.com/skybrary
https://apps.apple.com/us/app/levar-burton-kids-skybrary/id512350210

Section 14 Reading Websites

Listed below are a number of very good apps that will add a new tool or tools to your classroom. All of these reading apps get good reviews and are used by a number of people in the field. I recommend that you try some of them.

Epic! - Unlimited Books for Kids Honorable Mention
This is an eBook subscription service for educators and parents. The service is free for teachers and librarians. The service also has a number of books that can be read to you. That is very helpful if you are looking for books for someone with a disability related to reading print material.
https://www.getepic.com/educators
https://www.getepic.com/
https://itunes.apple.com/us/app/epic-unlimited-books-for-kids/id719219382?mt=8&ign-mpt=uo%3D4
https://chrome.google.com/webstore/detail/epic-unlimited-books-for/lmjefjipbldpocmjmmaljbjcnpepmooi?hl=en-US

Unite for Literacy
This website has a number of free online books for younger readers.
https://www.uniteforliteracy.com/

Newsela Honorable Mention
This website will adjust reading levels for the same article. This means that students on different reading levels can read the same article.
https://newsela.com/
Chrome: https://chrome.google.com/webstore/detail/newsela/bfpeiapdhnegnfcfkdfihabadngjagfj?utm_source=chrome-ntp-icon

TweenTribune
This is a free reading website for teachers.
http://tweentribune.com/

GCFLearnFree.org
This website has a number of free activities to help improves skills. The website gets some good reviews.
https://edu.gcfglobal.org/en/

COMMONLIT
This website is free and tracks student's progress when reading.
https://www.commonlit.org/

READTHEORY
This is a free website that gives you data on your student's progress.
https://readtheory.org/

Starfall
This website is for young children learning to read. The website has a number of free materials.
https://www.starfall.com/h/index-grades123.php

Read Works
This website has a number of articles that are supported by audio and has other materials.
https://www.readworks.org/

Rewordify
This is a great tool to simplify text to different reading levels. It also helps make the text easier to understand.
https://rewordify.com/

Storyline Online
This website has a number of children's story that is read to you on video.
https://www.storylineonline.net/

Section 15 Reading iPad Apps

News-O-Matic, Daily Reading for Kids Honorable Mention
You can find the same article on three different reading
levels with this app. It is a very popular reading app with
good reviews.
https://itunes.apple.com/us/app/news-o-matic-daily-
reading/id578023255?mt=8&ign-mpt=uo%3D4

News-O-Matic EDU, Nonfiction Reading Honorable
Mention
This app gives you five easy reading high-interest stories
per day to promote reading.
https://itunes.apple.com/us/app/news-o-matic-edu-
nonfiction-reading/id905215549?mt=8&ign-mpt=uo%3D4

HOMER Reading: Learn To Read Honorable Mention
This is a popular online reading program that is accessed
via an app. The program customizes learning for each
student. That means each student gets a personized learning
experience. The reviews are also outstanding.
https://itunes.apple.com/US/app/id601437586?mt=8
https://play.google.com/store/apps/details?id=com.learnwit
hhomer.webapp
Homer is free for
educators: https://learnwithhomer.com/teachers/funnel/
Free to try: https://learnwithhomer.com/onboarding

Insert Learning
With this website/Chrome extension, you can turn a webpage into a guided reading activity. This service would work well for a reading teacher. Insert Learning would work well for other subjects that require reading and answer questions about what you have read. There is a free version of the service and paid versions. I like the concept.
https://insertlearning.com
https://chrome.google.com/webstore/detail/insertlearning/dehajjkfchegiinhcmoclkfbnmpgcahj?hl=en

Fry Words Games and Flash Cards
This app has lists of the 1000 most common words. Using flashcards to teach the most common words is a great strategy to use with young children using to read. Using flashcards is a good way to help with memorization.
https://apps.apple.com/us/app/fry-words-games-and-flash-cards/id1031640659

ReadingIQ
You can find a ton of reading options based on ability and interest. If you are teaching reading and want comprehensive choices, this is a possibility. This is a free app with in-app purchases.
https://itunes.apple.com/us/app/readingiq/id1423345636?mt=8

I Like Stories - Storytime for Kids and Endless Readers
This app has a number of free stories for very young children. (age 0-6) You can also make in-app purchases.
https://apps.apple.com/us/app/i-like-stories-storytime-for-kids-and-endless-readers/id833461983

Endless Reader
This app teaches basic reading skills to young children by helping them learn common vocabulary. The app also gets high ratings.
https://itunes.apple.com/us/app/endless-reader/id722910739?mt=8

Reading Comprehension Prep
This is a highly rated reading app.
https://itunes.apple.com/us/app/reading-comprehension-prep/id739985631?mt=8

Immersive Reader
This program has a number of tools that help struggling readers.
https://www.microsoft.com/en-us/p/immersive-reader/9pjzqz821dq2?activetab=pivot:overviewtab

HOOKED - Chat Stories
This app gives you a story in the form of a series of text messages. There is research to suggest reading a few words at a time can improve reading. The concept the app is based on does create engagement. The story ends with a cliffhanger that you have to wait an hour to find the answer. Hence, the name hooked.
https://itunes.apple.com/us/app/hooked-chat-stories/id1024818709?mt=8
https://play.google.com/store/apps/details?id=tv.telepathic.hooked&hl=en

Oceanhouse Media
The website has a number of apps for Google or iTunes of very popular children's stories.
http://www.oceanhousemedia.com/apps/dr-seuss/
https://play.google.com/store/search?q=oceanhouse%20media%20%22dr.%20seuss%22

Section 16 Learning Ally

Learning Ally is a great service that is often underutilized. Imagine if you could listen to all of your textbooks. The number of students that would benefit from this service is a large number. The service does cost money, but it is much better than the alternative. As more textbooks are online and have electronic versions, the service might become less important in the future. Every device, browser, and operating system have speech to text options. The ability to listen to books is very powerful. For some students, the need to listen to textbooks is a real need. In the past, you needed an expensive digital player and access to the talking books was less streamlined. Today you can listen on any device, and the technical issues are far less. I cannot emphasize enough how great this service is. Learning Ally has a large collection of textbooks that can be listened to.

Learning Ally Link Chrome Honorable Mention
https://chrome.google.com/webstore/detail/learning-ally-link/gdicnpbaekbefjanokchpfhnaphfnphl?hl=en-US

Learning Ally Link PC
This is PC software that allows you to access Learning Ally.
http://rfbd.vo.llnwd.net/o41/applications/link/Windows/Learning%20Ally%20Link.msi

Learning Ally Link Mac
This is the Mac version of the software for Learning Ally.
https://itunes.apple.com/us/app/learning-ally-link/id906070888?mt=12

Learning Ally Link iPad
This app will allow you to listen to Learning Ally on an iPad or iPhone.
https://itunes.apple.com/us/app/learning-ally-link/id1131235021?mt=8

Learning Ally Google Play
You can use Learning Ally on a Chromebook or in the Chrome browser with this extension.
https://play.google.com/store/apps/details?id=org.learningally.LinkMobile&hl=en

Section 17 Advanced Grammar & Spell-Checkers

I find most spelling and grammar checks are disappointing. Having a spelling and grammar check is better than nothing. There are a number of mistakes that they do not find. Having a more well-developed grammar and spelling checker is a real need for many people. I find the best service is Grammarly. There are still a number of alternatives if you want to look elsewhere. As an adult that does a lot of writing, I don't want to ask others to proofread my work. Having electronic options to point out my mistakes is valuable.

Note: My brother works for Grammarly. I do really like my brother, but if a better product than Grammarly comes along, I will write about it.

Grammarly Best of Class Author's Pick
This website will make a ton of corrections on your work. There is a web browser version that will correct what you are writing and a Microsoft Word add-on. They also have a paid version. This is great for a college student or someone that needs help correcting their writing on a regular basis.
https://www.grammarly.com/
https://chrome.google.com/webstore/detail/grammarly-for-chrome/kbfnbcaeplbcioakkpcpgfkobkghlhen?hl=en

Microsoft Word
The spelling and grammar checker in Microsoft Word is very good. To ignore the strong spelling and grammar checking in Word for other programs is a mistake. If you use Word, enjoy the benefit of spelling and grammar checking. However, if you are a power-user, you still can supplement Word with another option as well.
https://www.microsoft.com/en-us/p/word/cfq7ttc0k7c7?activetab=pivot%3aoverviewtab

Language Tool
This is a tool that corrects your grammar, spelling and sentence structure. There is a simple free version to use and paid options. The tool as not as well known. The Language Tool gets some good reviews and has some nice features. What I like best is that you can try the product without login in, downloading or giving any information. The Language Tools also has a few browser extensions that you can try. If you are in the market for a tool to correct your writing, this is worth a look.
https://languagetool.org/
https://chrome.google.com/webstore/detail/grammar-and-spell-checker/oldceeleldhonbafppcapldpdifcinji
https://addons.mozilla.org/en-US/firefox/addon/languagetool/
https://appsource.microsoft.com/en-us/product/office/WA104381727?flightCodes=rezopia&tab=Overview

Ginger

This is an advanced spelling and grammar checker. You can get the free version or buy two paid versions. The company offers discounts for students and schools. The program starts up with your computer.

Website: http://www.gingersoftware.com/

Google

Play: https://play.google.com/store/apps/details?id=com.gingersoftware.android.keyboard&referrer=utm_source%3Dgingersoftware%26utm_medium%3Dwebsite_traffic%26utm_campaign%3Dandroid_keyboard_page_dl_button

Chrome: http://www.gingersoftware.com/extensions/chrome

Windows: http://www.gingersoftware.com/ginger-for-windows

Safari: http://www.gingersoftware.com/extensions/safari

Mac: https://itunes.apple.com/app/id822797943?id=com.gingersoftware.ios.keyboard&refferal=utm_source%3Dgingersoftware%26utm_medium%3Dwebsite_traffic%26utm_campaign%3Dginger_for_mac_dl_button

Ginger Page Writing App

This app helps you make corrections to your writing.

iPad: https://itunes.apple.com/us/app/ginger-page-writing-app-spell/id822797943?mt=8

Writable

This website gives added structure and feedback to your writing assignments. This a product integrates with Google Suite. If you are a Google School, then consider this product.

https://www.writable.com/

ProWriting Aid

This advanced spell checker has a number of features. The one I like is the one-year subscription is 40 dollars. The program will check for many different qualities in your writing, and it integrates with Google Documents and Word.

https://prowritingaid.com/

Hemingway Editor

This online editor gives you feedback on your writing. There are several advantages to using this editor. It is free, you do not have to install software, and you can use it with your entire class. This editor gives you more considerable feedback compared to a word processor.

http://www.hemingwayapp.com/

http://www.hemingwayapp.com/help.html

Section 18 Writing Help

WriteWell Online Hidden Gem
The website is excellent. You can access a number of
online templates from this website/Chrome extension. The
Chrome extension has a number of templates to help
organize writing and help with basic editing. This extension
gets very good reviews as well. This is a hidden gem.
https://chrome.google.com/webstore/detail/writewell-
online/obkdedbflcnbpillohfoghmjpekelpek?hl=en-US
https://writewellapp.com/

IELTS Essays
This app help students with structuring an essay. This is a
very important school for students with organizational
issues or struggling writers. The focus of this is on writing
structure, not writing mechanics.
https://apps.apple.com/us/app/ielts-essays/id1185022529

Power Thesaurus
This is a tool form someone that does a lot of writing that
needs to use a variety of words. If you are writing a number
of reports that require you to say information in your own
words a quality thesaurus is a must.
https://chrome.google.com/webstore/detail/power-
thesaurus/hhnjkanigjoiglnlopahbbjdbfhkndjk?hl=en

As a writer, I constantly look up spelling, grammar, and
vocabulary. It is a good habit to get into. With spell-check
and grammar check students are more likely to overlook
the need for this. Websites on grammar are a great way to
give examples of grammar. If your goal is to increase your
students' grammar skills, then this is something you want
to consider. Grammar websites allow the student to teach
themselves with multiple ways of having a concept

represented. If you project one of these websites, it can be a strong visual to represent common instances of correct grammar or common grammar mistakes. There are also advanced spelling and grammar checkers. The one I use is Grammarly.

The Purdue Online Writing Lab OWL Honorable Mention
This is an outstanding website if you want to look up or understand grammar.
https://owl.english.purdue.edu/

Grammar Girl
This is a popular grammar website.
http://www.quickanddirtytips.com/grammar-girl

Section 19 Learn to Spelling

There are a number of ways to teach spelling. I want to make a few suggestions. When you are teaching spelling to young children, you have to teach phonics and the parts of a word. You can find lists of the most commonly used 100 words. Every child should know how to spell all of those words. Memorizing letters within a word can be a mundane task. Anytime that you find a way to make this task more interesting or better target common words that is a win. I recommend looking at the options below.

Scholar - Spelling Bee Quiz
This app teaches you to spell commonly misspelled words. It gets into similar words. The ratings are excellent and well deserved. This is a difficult subject to address. This app will help you improve your spelling if you take the time to use it.
https://itunes.apple.com/us/app/scholar-spelling-bee-quiz/id1308540467

Spelling Training
This website allows you to make a list of spelling words or import one to study. This is a nice twist to the traditional way of learning spelling.
https://www.spellingtraining.com/

Spelling Notebook
You can create a list of spelling words to practice. This app helps teach spelling.
https://itunes.apple.com/us/app/spelling-notebook/id461225509?mt=8

Simplex Spelling Phonics - Rhyming With CVC Words
This is a very good spelling app.
https://itunes.apple.com/us/app/simplex-spelling-phonics-rhyming/id580762950?mt=8&ign-mpt=uo%3D4
Website: http://www.pyxwise.com/ssphonicscvc.html

Little Stars - Word Wizard
This is a highly rated game that teaches spelling.
https://itunes.apple.com/us/app/little-stars-word-wizard/id521736568?mt=8

Wonster Words Learning
This app teaches phonics and spelling. The app also gets great reviews.
https://apps.apple.com/us/app/wonster-words-learning/id881119321

Ultimate English Spelling Quiz
Google Play
https://play.google.com/store/apps/details?id=com.damtechdesigns.quiz.spelling&hl=en
Windows https://www.microsoft.com/en-us/store/apps/ultimate-english-spelling-quiz/9nblggh1r9ns

American Wordspeller
Instead of looking a word up in the dictionary, you can use this app. Spelling rules do not apply. You can spell a word phonctically, and the app can find it. This is an app for those with poor spelling that needs to look up a word.
https://itunes.apple.com/us/app/american-wordspeller/id397617771?mt=8

Spell Board

This app creates fun activities to help you learn custom spelling lists.

https://itunes.apple.com/us/app/spellboard/id390290951?mt=8

Website: http://www.palasoftware.com/SpellBoard.html

YouTube.com

You can find videos of the most common 100 words and countless videos on phonics. When I show videos to students, they just focus or listen better. As much as I want to think of myself as being interesting YouTube.com tends to be more engaging interesting to my students.

https://www.youtube.com/

Section 20 Autism Writing Guide

For students that are high functioning autism setting goals and expectations is very important. With good structure, we are proactive instead of reactive, and writing hit on a number of weaknesses that high functioning autism students have. There are deficits in language, lack of understanding of social information that translates to difficulty in creative writing. Often times students with autism do not like the act of handwriting. Some of that is language based. In many cases, they have difficulty with the fine motor coordination that is required for writing. When you tell students to write a story about what you did this weekend often time students with autism do not know what to write or why others would be interested, this same problem can translate to creative writing. It can be the case they do not understand the purpose of the activity. Having a checklist of some basic expectation will make it more likely that they do the work. This kind of communication can give meaning to what they do and help them to understand what work to do.

There are many checklist applications to pick from. I choose one to get started. If you just make a list in Google Documents and share it with them, that is okay as well.

Wunderlist – To-Do & Task List Honorable Mention
This is a very popular to-do-list app. There is also a website that you can access as well.
https://itunes.apple.com/us/app/wunderlist-to-do-task-list/id406644151?mt=8&ign-mpt=uo%3D4
Website: https://www.wunderlist.com/en/
https://play.google.com/store/apps/details?id=com.wunderkinder.wunderlistandroid&hl=en

Writing Ideas Generators and Prompts
The Writer's Plot Generator
http://writers-den.pantomimepony.co.uk/writers-plot-ideas.php

Story Picture Inspiration
https://www.pinterest.com/explore/story-inspiration/

Visual Writing Prompts
http://visualprompts.weebly.com/high-school.html

Journal Writing Prompts
http://www.dailyteachingtools.com/journal-writing-prompts.html

365 Writing Prompts
http://thinkwritten.com/365-creative-writing-prompts/

Write About This
You ever get students that can't find something to write about? This app is filled with many writing prompts. This app is highly rated.
https://itunes.apple.com/us/app/write-about-this/id601375313?mt=8

Word Banks

This might seem like a strange idea for writing. However, if you give a word bank of vocabulary and ask the students to use each, word, you are creating structure. The question they will ask out loud or to themselves is, "how will I do this?" The answer is to write a topic sentence then put each word into a sentence. You can give different students different words. Try giving them five words and having them writes a paragraph. Sometimes setting small goals and getting them started is the most important thing to do.

Peer Story Telling

We do peer editing why not storytelling? Have students work in groups of two. Each student has to tell the basic story in a short time frame. If one student does not have an idea for the story, then have that specific student listen to someone that has a story to tell. The other student will model an example of a story. They will ask each other several questions. The questions they ask will be almost the same questions you would ask them. Some people think out loud better than in isolation. It is a good trick to break writer block. The movement within the classroom will benefit some of your students as well.

Alternative Story Telling

Have them draw a picture, act out a scene or make a short video. Even just filling out a storyboard with stick figures and sharing and explaining with a peer can make a big difference. This creates movement and can calm some people and give them a short break from a lower interest activity. You can structure the activity so that it is short. Try using a timer. Think about it as a constructive break for the student that is aligned with the curriculum. You should consider the right combination of students, limiting the time and most importantly make the activity fun. Teachers that use such creative ideas get noticed by peers in a positive way. Years ago, I did activities like this, and no one else was. I was able to engage students that had significant problems, and they enjoyed the activities. This can add a new dimension to your teaching. The best part is today that most teachers will like and understand why you are doing this.

Create Structured Writing Actives
I have taught writing, and I am a writer. You might find this surprising, but I did not like writing as a child. The fact that I am dyslexic, and several years behind in writing did not help. The truth is a good teacher can overcome this. The first thing we must do is stop making assumptions. Some people have a hard time making up a story and using descriptive language. We often just assume people can make up a story from thin air. It is hard to believe in a time with Netflix and internet videos that people exist that struggle to tell a story with creative writing.

I recommend structured writing assignments. This means you give them part of the story and write about what happens next. This might mean you give them a picture and have them write about what happens next. You can have them draw a picture and then write about it. You might want to be careful about using Mad-Libs with middle school students. The idea of leaving the students to figure it out is not a good option. This problem is real. The worst thing that can happen is it does not work. If you understand that as a teacher, you can be creative and make the problem smaller and more manageable is the right move.

Graphic Organizers

Google Keep Author's Pick
I would recommend using Google Keep as a graphic organizer if you use Google Documents.
https://www.google.com/keep/

WriteWell Online Hidden Gem
The website is excellent. You can access a number of online templates from this website/Chrome extension. The Chrome extension has a number of templates to help organize writing and help with basic editing. This extension gets very good reviews as well. This is a hidden gem.
https://chrome.google.com/webstore/detail/writewell-online/obkdedbflcnbpillohfoghmjpekelpek?hl=en-US
https://writewellapp.com/

Specific Graphic Organizers
Characters:
http://www.fcrr.org/curriculum/PDF/G4-5/45CPartOne.pdf
https://www.pinterest.com/explore/character-traits-graphic-organizer/
http://bcs.schoolwires.net/cms/lib5/AL01001646/Centricity/Domain/131/Common%20Core%20Graphic%20Organizers%20for%20Literature%20Standards%20Grade%205.pdf
http://www.literacyleader.com/sites/default/files/Character%20Graphic%20Organizers.pdf
https://www.risd.k12.nm.us/assessment_evaluation/Character%20Analysis.pdf

Setting
http://www.eduref.org/Virtual/Lessons/Language_Arts/Writing/WCP0222e.pdf

Writing a Paragraph or Essay:
https://www.superteacherworksheets.com/graphic-organizers/hamburger-writing_WBRDM.pdf

SmartDraw
This is a software program that helps you draw graphic organizers and colorful diagrams. This program is for someone that wants to write curriculum.
https://www.smartdraw.com/education/examples/

Story Boards:
http://www.scholastic.com/teachers/sites/default/files/asset/file/story-board-reading-comprehension-graphic-organizer.pdf
http://edselect.com/Docs/Graphicorganizers.pdf
http://www.balancedreading.com/graphorg.pdf

Write About This
This is a highly rated, dynamic writing prompt app for elementary school.
https://itunes.apple.com/us/app/write-about-this/id601375313?mt=8&ign-mpt=uo%3D4

Word Prediction

Read & Write (Chrome Extension) Best of Class
This Chrome extension has just about everything. Read & Write has word prediction that is excellent. The app has a picture dictionary. The extension has speech to text and text to speech. The app creates a floating toolbar in the Chrome browser. This means a student can use Read & Write across all settings. It also means that a student can use Read & Write on any computer. That can eliminate the need for a laptop to travel with the student. It also means that a student could use this product at home with no extra cost or risk on the part of the school. The subscription is priced on the number of licenses purchased. The more licenses purchased, the less per license.
https://chrome.google.com/webstore/detail/readwrite-for-google-chro/inoeonmfapjbbkmdafoankkfajkcphgd
A teacher can get this extension for free. This allows teachers to test out the product.
https://www.texthelp.com/en-us/products/read-write/free-for-teachers/

Voice Dream Writer Honorable Mention
This is a very good word prediction app. The app will type what you say. All you do is click on the microphone on the keyboard. It also makes some basic corrections. The app will even read back what you typed. This is an awesome app.
https://itunes.apple.com/us/app/voice-dream-writer/id920583100?mt=8
Website http://www.voicedream.com/writer/

Word Q US 1 (Chrome)

This is a very good word prediction app.

https://chrome.google.com/webstore/detail/wordq-us-i/pojcommghdpcglmnodkpcdiknjfcgoge

Typing for Students with Greater Physical Limitations

Google Documents' Voice Typing Best of Class Hidden Gem Author's Pick Game Changer

Google Documents, also known as Google Docs, has speech to text that is free. Most humans have a Gmail account these days. Most people with disabilities and people that work with them have this great free technology already. What you should do is buy a headset with a microphone. I recommend one that connects with a USB port.

https://support.google.com/docs/answer/4492226?hl=en

Abilipad

This has to be one of the most interesting apps I have ever encountered. It is text to speech, customizable keyboard, and word prediction. If you have trouble spelling and talking this app would be a good fit. You can even create a keyboard exactly the way you want it. The app has several different things going on and as a result, is hard to place in a category.

https://itunes.apple.com/us/app/abilipad/id435865000?mt=8

Advanced Grammar and Spell Checkers

Grammarly Best of Class Author's Pick
This website will make a ton of corrections on your work. There is a web browser version that will correct what you are writing and a Microsoft Word add-on. They also have a paid version. This is great for a college student or someone that needs help correcting their writing on a regular basis.
https://www.grammarly.com/
https://chrome.google.com/webstore/detail/grammarly-for-chrome/kbfnbcaeplbcioakkpcpgfkobkghlhen?hl=en

Language Tool
This is a tool that corrects your grammar, spelling and sentence structure. There is a simple free version to use and paid options. The tool as not as well known. The Language Tool gets some good reviews and has some nice features. What I like best is that you can try the product without login in, downloading or giving any information. The Language Tools also has a few browser extensions that you can try. If you are in the market for a tool to correct your writing, this is worth a look.
https://languagetool.org/
https://chrome.google.com/webstore/detail/grammar-and-spell-checker/oldceeleldhonbafppcapldpdifcinji
https://addons.mozilla.org/en-US/firefox/addon/languagetool/
https://appsource.microsoft.com/en-us/product/office/WA104381727?flightCodes=rezopia&tab=Overview

Section 21 Pen Readers/Recorder for Notes

Pen readers are a great idea that people often forget about in the world of software. We think of hardware for people with more significant disabilities. You can buy a pen that reads print text. Online text is accessible and paper text is not. With a pen reader, the truth is paper text can be read to you.

Livescribe records notes and syncs them to what you write. This is a great tool for students. With all of the options out there sometimes people forget this option.

Livescribe
This is a pen that syncs a person's voice to the notes that are taken. The notes and audio are then turned into a video. This pen is used for someone with a disability. However, I like this pen for teachers trying to create a lesson. This is one way to flip a classroom.
http://www.livescribe.com/en-us/

C-Pen Reader
This pen will scan in paper text and read it to you in real time. You scan one line at a time.
http://www.scanningpens.com/?fmprompt=false

LeapReader from LeapFrog
You can read and write with a pen. The pen reads the words or can be used for practicing basic writing. The company has a number of products for teaching literacy skills. The products get some very good reviews. The Company has a number of other products that teach reading as well.
https://www.leapfrog.com/en-us/store/p/leapreader-reading-and-writing-system/_/A-prod21301

Section 22 Preschool Curriculum Apps

Draw and Tell HD - by Duck Duck Moose
This is a drawing app for preschoolers. The app allows
young children to tell a story and create a picture.
https://itunes.apple.com/us/app/draw-tell-hd-by-duck-
duck/id504752087?mt=8

Big City Vehicles - Cars and Trucks for Kids
This is a highly rated educational game for preschoolers
and toddlers.
https://itunes.apple.com/us/app/big-city-vehicles-cars-and-
trucks-for-kids/id997799804?mt=8&ign-mpt=uo%3D4

PrestoBingo Shapes - Puzzle & Counting Game for
Preschool to Kindergarten Kids
This highly rated app teaches about shapes and numbers.
https://itunes.apple.com/us/app/prestobingo-shapes-puzzle-
counting-game-for-preschool/id494347130?mt=8&ign-
mpt=uo%3D4

My PlayHome Stores
This app lets you play with real world items
https://itunes.apple.com/us/app/my-playhome-
stores/id683942610?mt=8

MarcoPolo Ocean
This app is a fun way to get a young child interested in the
ocean.
https://itunes.apple.com/us/app/marcopolo-
ocean/id797157312?mt=8&ign-mpt=uo%3D4

Gus on the Go: Spanish for Kids
This app teaches Spanish.
https://itunes.apple.com/us/app/gus-on-the-go-spanish-for-kids/id541567964?mt=8

Gus on the Go: French for Kids
This app teaches French.
https://itunes.apple.com/us/app/gus-on-the-go-french-for-kids/id578992727?mt=8

Gus on the Go
You can teach 26 different languages with this series of apps.
http://www.gusonthego.com/gus-on-the-go-languages/

Preschool and Kindergarten Learning Games
The app teaches a variety of things within a preschool curriculum.
https://itunes.apple.com/us/app/preschool-kindergarten-learning/id509771809?mt=8&ign-mpt=uo%3D2
Website: http://www.kevinbradford.org/

Bug Mazing - Adventures in Learning
This highly rated app teaches the preschool curriculum.
https://itunes.apple.com/us/app/bug-mazing-adventures-in-learning/id879566736?mt=8&ign-mpt=uo%3D4

My Shapes & Colors Farm Puzzles - The free funny forms learning puzzle app for babies and toddlers
This app teaches about shapes and colors. The app gets good ratings.
https://itunes.apple.com/us/app/my-shapes-colors-farm-puzzles-free-funny-forms-learning/id912512580?mt=8&ign-mpt=uo%3D4

Preschool Games - Farm Animals by Photo Touch
You can learn about farm animals with this highly rated app.
https://itunes.apple.com/us/app/preschool-games-farm-animals-by-photo-touch/id439478226?mt=8

Animal Circus: Learning Games
This app has a ton of learning games and activities.
https://itunes.apple.com/us/app/animal-circus-learning-games/id510551395?mt=8

Shape-O ABC's
This is a highly rated game app that uses shapes to complete puzzles of pictures. This is a very good preschool app.
https://itunes.apple.com/us/app/shape-o-abcs/id415766828?mt=8&ign-mpt=uo%3D4

Toddler Learning Games Ask Me Color & Shape Games
This highly rated app teaches preschoolers about shapes and colors.
https://itunes.apple.com/us/app/toddler-learning-games-ask-me-color-shape-games/id689592594?mt=8

Imagination Box
This is a highly rated app from a very good app maker. It also teaches the basic information that preschoolers should learn.
https://itunes.apple.com/us/app/imagination-box-creative-fun/id698092635?mt=8

Toddler Marine Preschool - Educational Fish Games for Kids
This app has six mini-games for preschoolers.
https://itunes.apple.com/us/app/id563513035?mt=8
Website: http://www.polygonplay.com/kids-fish-game

Bugs and Buttons
This app is 18 games that teach many different things within the preschool curriculum.
https://itunes.apple.com/us/app/bugs-and-buttons/id446031868?mt=8

Bugs and Buttons 2
The app has 18 games that teach many different things within the preschool curriculum.
https://itunes.apple.com/app/bugs-and-buttons-2/id686968315?ls=1&mt=8

Alien Buddies – Preschool Learning Activities
The app is based on the basic preschool curriculum. You learn colors, shapes, letters, and numbers. This app puts a high-interest spin on learning.
https://itunes.apple.com/us/app/alien-buddies-preschool-learning/id469461540?mt=8

Barnyard Games For Kids
This game is based on the preschool curriculum. That includes colors, shapes, numbers, and letters.
https://itunes.apple.com/us/app/barnyard-games-for-kids/id498685080?mt=8

Section 23 Math for Preschool and Kindergarten

Endless Numbers
This app teaches young children about numbers and basic math.
https://itunes.apple.com/us/app/endless-numbers/id804360921?mt=8

The Math Tree
This is a fun game app that teaches very basic math skills. The app also gets some very good reviews.
https://itunes.apple.com/us/app/the-math-tree/id587028310?mt=8

Animal Pre-K Math and Early Learning Games for Kids in Preschool and Kindergarten Free
This app follows Common Core standards. The app teaches basic preschool and Kindergarten skills.
https://itunes.apple.com/us/app/animal-pre-k-math-early-learning-games-for-kids-in/id882334694?mt=8

Animal Math Games for Kids in Pre-K, Kindergarten and 1st Grade Learning Numbers, Counting, Addition and Subtraction Free
This app teaches the basic operation in a high-interest way.
https://itunes.apple.com/us/app/animal-math-games-for-kids-in-pre-k-kindergarten-1st/id799973028?mt=8

Todo K-2 Math Practice
This app has eight games to teach addition, subtraction, and counting of numbers. This app uses high-interest activities to teach math.
https://itunes.apple.com/us/app/todo-k-2-math-practice/id666465255?mt=8&ign-mpt=uo%3D4

Sums Stacker
This app teaches you the value of numbers.
https://itunes.apple.com/us/app/sums-stacker/id343251346?mt=8

Counting Money Apps

TallyTots Counting
This app has a number of different games that teaches basic counting.
https://itunes.apple.com/us/app/tallytots-counting/id424070269?mt=8

Counting Dots - Preschoolers Learn To Count
This is a highly rated app that teaches a preschooler to count.
https://itunes.apple.com/us/app/counting-dots-preschoolers-learn-to-count/id484775327?mt=8

The Lonely Beast 123 - Preschool Number Counting
This app teaches basic counting to preschoolers, and it gets very good ratings.
https://itunes.apple.com/us/app/the-lonely-beast-123-preschool-number-counting/id646406000?mt=8&ign-mpt=uo%3D4

Telling Time Apps

Interactive Telling Time - Learning to tell time is fun. This is a fun app to help people learn to tell time. http://itunes.apple.com/us/app/interactive-telling-time-learning/id477389150?mt=8

Section 24 Behavior

Behavior is one of the most important aspects of teaching. If a child does not behave, then learning can stop or become much more difficult. We tend to notice behavior when it is disruptive and impacts learning. When we can do something to improve behavior, we always should at least try. There are a number of apps that can help you track behavior. This can remind us of how important behavior is, and hopefully, it reminds us to make adjustments as parents and teachers. It can also help us to create a good structure to maintain good behavior and prevent problems later on.

Schedule Apps

Choiceworks Honorable Mention
This is a very good app to make a simple visual schedule.
https://itunes.apple.com/us/app/choiceworks/id486210964?mt=8

Class Timetable
You can keep track of all your assignments with this app. It is designed for a high school or college student that has a lot going on.
https://itunes.apple.com/us/app/class-timetable/id425121147?mt=8

Happy Kids Timer
This timer helps to get young children to complete everyday tasks. This would also work well with children that have some forms of autism.
https://itunes.apple.com/us/app/happy-kids-timer-morning-routines-education-motivation/id978996118?mt=8&ign-mpt=uo%3D4

Behavior Tracking

Autism Tracker Pro: Track and Analyze ASD
This app helps you keep a schedule and helps you keep track of behaviors. It comes with too many tools to describe in a few sentences.
https://itunes.apple.com/us/app/autism-tracker-pro-track-and-analyze-asd/id478225574?mt=8&ign-mpt=uo%3D4

TrackCC
This app is designed for teachers or administrators to keep track of attendance, grades and other important data about students.
https://itunes.apple.com/us/app/trackcc/id924533158?mt=8

Management and Reinforcement

PECS Phase III
You get immediate feedback when a student gets a right answer, and it is designed to reinforce the behavior. I love the concept.
https://itunes.apple.com/us/app/pecs-phase-iii/id551356825?mt=8

Lickety Split

This app helps you set goals and time limits on desirable behaviors. If you want your child to clean his or her room, this app gives you a timer. If a child needs constant structure and time limits this is a good choice.
https://itunes.apple.com/us/app/lickety-split/id454354262?mt=8

Monitoring Student Devices

GoGradian

This software allows you to monitor the activity of students on Chromebooks.
https://www.goguardian.com/

ClassHub

ClassHub is software to monitor student's devices on different platforms.
http://www.airsquirrels.com/classhub/

Chapter 4 Occupational Therapy

What technologies are there for occupational therapy or for an occupational therapist to offer to students that have disabilities?

Physical Keyboards
This is a keyboard that is hardware.

Keyboard Apps or Programs
These are electronic keyboards. This can be an app for an iPad or a program that creates a keyboard for a computer.

Annotation Programs
This is a program that allows you to write or type on PDFs or pictures. This is helpful for people with fine motor coordination issues.

Exercise Apps
These are apps that have you do exercises to improve fine motor coordination.

Typing Programs
These are programs that have you practice typing or keyboarding skills.

Sensory Issues

Sensory issues are related to the senses. This is typically associated with autism spectrum disorders. However, an individual can have sensory issues without having a form of autism. This can be anything related to the senses. This can mean eating food, sound, visual, and definably tactile.

Section 1 Annotations

Annotations are marks that you put on top of a document. With a tablet or a computer, you can take a picture of a document then put marks on it. That could mean text or handwriting in different colors. It could also mean highlights or notes.

iPad Annotations Apps

SnapType Pro Best of Class Author's Pick
With this app, you take a picture of a document and then type on a picture of the document. The fact that this app streamlines the process makes it an awesome app.
https://itunes.apple.com/us/app/snaptype-pro/id1124123246?mt=8
https://play.google.com/store/apps/details?id=com.snaptypeapp.android.pro
http://www.snaptypeapp.com/

iAnnotate 4 — PDFs & more
This is an annotation app that gets some good ratings.
https://apps.apple.com/us/app/iannotate-4-pdfs-more/id1093924230

ClaroPDF
This is a free annotation app with some very good reviews.
https://itunes.apple.com/us/app/claropdf/id666770153

GoodReader PDF Editor & Viewer
This is an annotation app that is also good at organization.
The app has been around for a long time and gets some
good ratings.
https://apps.apple.com/us/app/goodreader-pdf-editor-
viewer/id777310222

PDF Expert by Readdle
This is a highly rated annotation app.
https://itunes.apple.com/us/app/pdf-expert-6-read-annotate-
edit-pdf-documents/id743974925?mt=8

ClaroPDF Pro
This is a paid annotation app with some good reviews.
https://apps.apple.com/us/app/claropdf-pro/id633997623

Chrome

Kami Extension - PDF and Document Annotation
This is a highly rated annotation extension.
https://chrome.google.com/webstore/detail/kami-extension-
pdf-and-do/ecnphlgnajanjnkcmbpancdjoidceilk?hl=en

Google Play Annotations Apps

Diigo
This is an organization and annotation tool. The website helps you keep bookmarks. You can also annotate PDFs.
https://www.diigo.com/
https://chrome.google.com/webstore/detail/diigo-web-collector-captu/pnhplgjpclknigjpccbcnmicgcieojbh?hl=en
https://play.google.com/store/apps/details?id=com.diigo.android&hl=en

Xodo PDF Reader & Editor
This app annotates PDFs and open Word documents.
https://play.google.com/store/apps/details?id=com.xodo.pdf.reader
https://itunes.apple.com/us/app/xodo-pdf-pro-highlight-sign-search-take-notes-edit/id805075929?mt=8

Annotations
This app allows you to label important notes with different colors. It helps you stay organized.
https://play.google.com/store/apps/details?id=com.mv.notas&hl=en

Section 2 OT Exercise

Dexteria Author's Pick
This has games and different exercises that help strengthen your fingers. The program helps develop fine motor coordination.
http://itunes.apple.com/us/app/dexteria-fine-motor-skill/id420464455?mt=8

Dexteria Jr. - Fine Motor Skill Development
A preschooler can do exercises with this app. When you ask for the same task on an iPad and not with pencil and paper with younger students, you tend to get better results.
https://itunes.apple.com/us/app/dexteria-jr-fine-motor-skill-development/id624918435

Dexteria VMI Visual-Motor Integration Skills
This app has you put shapes in order.
https://itunes.apple.com/us/app/dexteria-vmi-visual-motor-integration-skills/id994021869

Dexteria Dots 2 - Fine Motor Skills and Math Concepts
This sequel will teach math concepts and fine motor coordination.
https://itunes.apple.com/us/app/dexteria-dots-2-fine-motor-skills-and-math-concepts/id899404716

Dexteria Dots - Get in Touch with Math
This app is a great way to practice fine motor coordination and math concepts.
https://itunes.apple.com/us/app/dexteria-dots-get-in-touch-with-math/id815345306

OverColor
You pick different colors and patterns that get more complex. This is a very interesting app.
https://itunes.apple.com/us/app/overcolor/id695133496?mt=8&ign-mpt=uo%3D4

Matrix Game 3
This app teaches visual perceptual skills.
https://itunes.apple.com/us/app/matrix-game-3/id468021471?mt=8

P.O.V. - Spatial Reasoning Skills Development
The app is designed for ages 8-18. You have to read the description in the app store to understand the different features. The app is highly rated. This app is made by the same app developer as Dexteria.
https://itunes.apple.com/us/app/p.o.v.-spatial-reasoning-skills/id532611500?mt=8&ign-mpt=uo%3D4

Ready to Print
This app was written by an occupational therapist to teach pre-writing skills.
https://itunes.apple.com/us/app/ready-to-print/id513780564?mt=8

Injini: Child Development Game Suite
This app teaches basic language and fine motor skills to young children.
https://itunes.apple.com/us/app/injini-child-development-game/id452962000?mt=8&ign-mpt=uo%3D4

Cookie Doodle

This app allows students to work on fine motor coordination while making imaginary cookies. https://itunes.apple.com/us/app/cookie-doodle/id342128086?mt=8

Section 3 Practice Handwriting

LetterSchool - Block Letters Honorable Mention
The LetterSchool app is a very popular app to teacher letter formation.
https://itunes.apple.com/us/app/letterschool-block-letters/id435476174?mt=8
https://play.google.com/store/apps/details?id=com.letterschool&hl=en_US
http://www.letterschool.org/

LetterSchool - Learn to Write! Honorable Mention
This is an excellent app to teach basic letter formations.
https://itunes.apple.com/us/app/letterschool-learn-to-write/id481067676?mt=8

Handwriting Wizard - Learn to Write Letters, Numbers & Words
This highly rated app teaches you to write letters, numbers, and basic words.
https://itunes.apple.com/us/app/handwriting-wizard-learn-to/id1071890681?mt=8
https://play.google.com/store/apps/details?id=com.lescapadou.tracingfree&hl=en
https://play.google.com/store/apps/details?id=com.lescapadou.tracing&hl=en

iTrace — handwriting for kids
This a good app for tracing letters and improving letter formation.
https://itunes.apple.com/us/app/itrace-handwriting-for-kids/id583678381?mt=8&ign-mpt=uo%3D4

Writing Wizard - Kids Learn to Write Letters, Alphabet & Words
This app teaches you the letter by having you trace them. The app gets outstanding ratings as well.
https://itunes.apple.com/us/app/writing-wizard-kids-learn-to-write-letters-alphabet-words/id631446426?mt=8&ign-mpt=uo%3D4
https://play.google.com/store/apps/details?id=com.lescapadou.tracingfree&hl=en
https://www.amazon.com/Writing-Wizard-Premium-Learn-Letters/dp/B00QH32FUM/ref=pd_sim_405_6?_encoding=UTF8&psc=1&refRID=PTZ0RBYEYVCTJMVZHPEH

Ready to Print
This app was written by an occupational therapist to teach pre-writing skills.
https://itunes.apple.com/us/app/ready-to-print/id513780564?mt=8

StartDOT Handwriting
This is a very good handwriting app.
https://itunes.apple.com/us/app/startdot-handwriting/id653836151?mt=8&ign-mpt=uo%3D4

Cursive Writing

Cursive Writing Wizard
This app teaches you to write the basic letters.
https://itunes.apple.com/us/app/cursive-writing-wizard/id757843896?mt=8
https://play.google.com/store/apps/details?id=com.lescapadou.cursivefree&hl=en
https://www.amazon.com/Cursive-Writing-Wizard-Premium-Letters/dp/B00QH4RX9E/ref=pd_sim_405_1?_encoding=UTF8&psc=1&refRID=RD0XKHD1RSHD2T79A7BZ

Section 4 Typing

Freetypinggame.net Author's Pick
This is a fun website that teaches typing.
http://www.freetypinggame.net/

Interactive Site for Education (Typing)
This is a website with a number of games that teaches typing skills.
http://interactivesites.weebly.com/typing.html

TypingClub
This is a very highly rated Chrome extension that teaches typing.
https://chrome.google.com/webstore/detail/typingclub/obdb gibnhfcjmmpfijkpcihjieedpfah?hl=en

EduTyping
This is a typing program that is free to try, but you have to pay for the full version.
https://www.edutyping.com/

Typist
This is a typing program for a Mac computer.
Mac
https://itunes.apple.com/us/app/typist/id415166115?mt=12

Keyboarding without Tears
This is a typing website that is designed to teach students typing skills. I know people that really like this program.
http://www.hwtears.com/kwt
Google
Play: https://play.google.com/store/apps/details?id=air.com.hwtears.KeyboardingWithoutTears&hl=en
Chrome: https://chrome.google.com/webstore/detail/keyboarding-without-tears/majdlmcobepphgemnhehmohfkkldbmmm?hl=en
https://apps.apple.com/us/app/keyboarding-without-tears/id895423963

TapTyping
This app teaches you how to type. This app has a free version and a paid version.
https://itunes.apple.com/us/app/taptyping-typing-trainer/id376526006?mt=8
https://itunes.apple.com/us/app/taptyping-typing-trainer-suite/id364237969?mt=8

Typing Lessons
This is a Chrome extension that teaches typing skills.
https://chrome.google.com/webstore/detail/typing-lessons/heehkcnmhmdicclbnofindfmokhfnjag?hl=en

Section 5 Keyboards Apps

Keeble - Accessible keyboard
This app has a number of good features for students with physical limitations. The word prediction is very good for a wide range of students that struggle with writing.
https://itunes.apple.com/us/app/keeble-accessible-keyboard/id918497054?mt=8

Keedogo Plus - Keyboard for education
This is a keyboard that is for students of a younger age. The keyboard comes with word prediction, and the keyboard is easier to see if you have vision issues.
https://itunes.apple.com/us/app/keedogo-plus-keyboard-for/id918496636?mt=8

Keedogo - Keyboard for preschool
This keyboard makes it easier for your average preschooler.
https://itunes.apple.com/us/app/keedogo-keyboard-for-preschool/id915829477?mt=8

Abilipad
This has to be one of the most interesting apps I have ever encountered. It is text to speech, customizable keyboard, and word prediction. If you have trouble spelling and talking this app would be a good fit.
https://itunes.apple.com/us/app/abilipad/id435865000?mt=8

Big Keys Low Vision Keyboard
This is a good keyboard for someone with low vision.
https://itunes.apple.com/us/app/high-visibility-keyboard/id1139220959?mt=8

Section 6 iPad Keyboards

iKBC CD108BT Wired + Wireless 2 in 1 Mechanical Keyboard with Cherry MX Brown Switch for iOS, Android, Windows and Mac (Bluetooth 3.0, PBT OEM Profile Keycaps, 108-Key, Navy Blue Color, ANSI/US)
Mechanical keyboards are a high-quality keyboard. This is a full keyboard including the number pad. This keyboard can be paired with different devices. The keyboard works with iOS, Android and Windows. You can use this keyboard with many different devices.
https://www.amazon.com/CD108BT-Wireless-Mechanical-Keyboard-Bluetooth/dp/B07F61DNJP/ref=sr_1_5?keywords=full+keyboard+ios&qid=1549742483&s=gateway&sr=8-5

MoKo Wireless Bluetooth Keyboard, Ultra-Thin Foldable Rechargeable Keyboard for iPhone, iPad 9.7, iPad pro, Fire HD 10, Compatible with All iOS, Android and Windows Tablets Smartphones Devices, Gray
This keyboard is portable, reasonably priced and has a good design. The keyboard is on a slight angle for comfort. The compact design is excellent for travel.
https://www.amazon.com/MoKo-Ultra-Thin-Rechargeable-Compatible-Smartphones/dp/B07BNB6R7G/ref=sr_1_6?keywords=full+keyboard+ios&qid=1549742483&s=gateway&sr=8-6

DICTOPRO D100 Wireless Bluetooth Keyboard Universal for Portable Tablets Smartphones iOS Windows Android Multi-Device Folding Small Ultra-Slim, Best Built-in Battery, Compact & Powerful Blue Tooth
This keyboard is compact and sells for a reasonable price
https://www.amazon.com/Bluetooth-Universal-Smartphones-Multi-Device-Ultra-Slim/dp/B072X931BP/ref=sr_1_1?keywords=keyboard+ios&qid=1549743050&s=gateway&sr=8-1

CHESONA Bluetooth Keyboard Ultra Slim Sliding Stand Universal Wireless Bluetooth Keyboard Compatible Apple iOS iPad Pro Mini Air iPhone, Android Galaxy Tab Smartphones, Windows PC
This is a good keyboard that does not fold at a reasonable price.
https://www.amazon.com/s?k=keyboard+ios&s=review-rank&qid=1549743043&ref=sr_st_review-rank

VicTsing Ultra-Slim Portable Bluetooth Keyboard, Wireless Keyboard for iOS (iPhone, iPad), Android, Windows, Mac Computer, Laptop, Tablet, Smartphone, and Other Bluetooth Enabled Devices, Silver
This is a very good keyboard for a great price.
https://www.amazon.com/VicTsing-Ultra-Slim-Portable-Bluetooth-Smartphone/dp/B07M6SW6SS/ref=sr_1_9?keywords=keyboard+case+ios&qid=1549743302&s=gateway&sr=8-9

iPad Keyboard Case for iPad 2018 (6th Gen) - iPad 2017 (5th Gen) - iPad Pro 9.7 - iPad Air 2 & 1 - Thin & Light - 360 Rotatable - Wireless/BT - Backlit 10 Color - iPad Case with Keyboard
This is a high quality keyboard-case.
https://www.amazon.com/iPad-Keyboard-Case-2018-6th/dp/B07H42YGLR/ref=sr_1_3?keywords=keyboard+case+ios&qid=1549743409&s=gateway&sr=8-3

Lauren S. Enders, MA, CCC-SLP on Pinterest.com is a very good place to start when looking at keyboards
https://www.pinterest.com/lasenders/ipad-keyboards-and-keyboard-cases/

Section 7 Sensory

Therapy Brushes
These brushes are used to calm down people with autism and sensory issues.
https://www.google.com/search?q=Therapy+Brushes&oq=Therapy+Brushes&aqs=chrome..69i57j0j69i60j0l3.1194j0j7&sourceid=chrome&ie=UTF-8

Fidget Cube
This cube is designed to help people with difficulty focusing and/or with sensory issues.
https://www.google.com/search?q=Therapy+Brushes&oq=Therapy+Brushes&aqs=chrome..69i57j0j69i60j0l3.1194j0j7&sourceid=chrome&ie=UTF-8#q=Fidget+cube

Stress Balls
This can help with stress or sensory issues.

Subsection 1 Sound

Hanging up the acoustic tiles to reduce sound is not a high technology solution. Sensitivity to sound is a sensory problem that is hard to fix and often ignored. Acoustic foam tile is not expensive to hang. The challenge is getting the foam to stick to the wall. By gluing on a plastic back, that is the size the tiles can be easily attached to the wall with sticky Velcro. Having spent the time to hang the tiles though several methods I can say this method works the best. The only flaw is that if you are in a school, the fire department will not like these tiles. However, as a parent, it solves a real problem. If hanging these tiles leads to a child sleeping, doing homework or not fighting with parents, the tiles are a big positive.

The way to hang the acoustic tiles is to glue clear plastic squares to the back of the tiles with regular glue. There is no need to buy a special type of glue. Once the plastic square is fixed to the tile, hang the tiles with sticky Velcro. The sticky Velcro will stick to the wall and plastic backing of the acoustic tile. Then, you arrange the tiles in the pattern you desire.

Acoustic Tiles

Foam Factory
This is where I purchased acoustic foam tiles at a good price.
https://www.foambymail.com/acoustical-foam-products.html

Grafix Clear Craft Plastic .007 Thickness 12-Inch by 12-Inch, Pack of 25
This is an inexpensive way to enable acoustic tiles to stick to a wall. If you use regular generic glue to attach this clear plastic square to the back of the tiles, they will hang quite nicely. The squares and tiles are the same sizes. I used sticky Velcro to attach them to the wall.
https://www.amazon.com/gp/product/B001K7Q6Z0/ref=ppx_yo_dt_b_asin_title_o03__o00_s00?ie=UTF8&psc=1

Elmer's Glue-All Multi-Purpose Liquid Glue, Extra Strong, 32 Ounces, 1 Count (E3850)
This is inexpensive glue that can be used to attach the plastic squares to acoustic tiles.
https://www.amazon.com/Elmers-Glue-All-Multi-Purpose-Liquid-E3850/dp/B0045PVK9Q/ref=sr_1_4?s=hi&ie=UTF8&qid=1548613207&sr=1-4&keywords=elmer%27s+glue

Duck Brand Self Adhesive Foam Weather-strip Seal for Extra Large Gaps, 3/4-Inch x 1/2-Inch x 10-Feet, 3 Rolls, 284424
These foam strips are used to insulate doors in a home. The insulation can also stop sound from passing through a door. This thick foam goes along the door jam. This does not have to seal the door to work. The idea is to have sound hit the foam on the way through the door. You do not have to seal the door.
https://www.amazon.com/gp/product/B00MZHXIY6/ref=ppx_yo_dt_b_asin_title_o08__o00_s00?ie=UTF8&psc=1

212

Foam Strips with Adhesive, High-Density Soundproofing
Window Insulation Foam Gasket Tape Weather Strip 1
Inch Wide X 1/8 Inch Thick X 33 Feet Long (1in 1/8in)
This thin foam goes between the door and the doorway.
This can prevent the door from making noise when
slamming. The foam does a great job of stopping sound
from coming through your door.
https://www.amazon.com/gp/product/B071RDDC2R/ref=p
px_yo_dt_b_asin_title_o08__o00_s00?ie=UTF8&psc=1

Velcro

Strenco 2 Inch Adhesive Black Hook and Loop Tape - 5
Yards - Heavy Duty - Sticky Back Fastener
This Velcro is very thick. That means it can hand and hold
up a lot of weight. That means the tile will stick and you
will not have to fix them later.
https://www.amazon.com/gp/product/B00H3R9S1K/ref=pp
x_yo_dt_b_asin_title_o04_s01?ie=UTF8&psc=1

Subsection 2 Food

I know food is not technology. However, if you have a child that has low muscle tone or has eating problems, weight issues or sensory related eating problems it is just as complicated. Understanding how to handle these issues takes technical knowledge similar to understanding technology. When I hear a child has low muscle tone, I cringe. Something as simple as drinking instant breakfast can help change this. People sometimes say you are what you eat. The truth is you are what you absorb. If someone has low muscle tone, a healthier diet would help. Now try getting a child to eat lean meats and vegetables is very difficult. If you have a child with sensory issues, it gets worse. Children with autism and learning disabilities often eat the mild tasting foods, and that can translate to a high carbohydrate diet. If you want to break this habit, it takes an educated parent with technological cooking knowledge. I can't understand why eating disorders for children with disabilities are not talked about and publicly recognized. Many parents are embarrassed by their children's maladaptive eating behaviors and blame themselves. Parents need to understand they are not to blame, and this needs to be talked about. I have listed some books below that will help parents struggling with this difficult problem.

Books

The Sneaky Chef: Simple Strategies for Hiding Healthy Foods in Kids' Favorite by Missy Chase Lapine

The Speedy Sneaky Chef: Quick, Healthy Fixes for Your Favorite Packaged Foods by Missy Chase Lapine

Deceptively Delicious: Simple Secrets to Get Your Kids Eating Good Food by Jessica Seinfeld

The Sneaky Chef to the Rescue: 101 All-New Recipes and "Sneaky" Tricks for Creating Healthy Meals Kids Will Love by Missy Chase Lapine

Nutrition

Instant Breakfast
I stock my home with Instant Breakfast. I prefer getting the version without sugar. As a child, I drank chocolate milk and these tastes just as good. What I find is when you buy similar products in a health food store they have more nutrition but don't taste as good. If people drink this every day, they will help you maintain or possible increase muscle tone. Some people have difficulty absorbing nutrients, and this can help you compensate. I have seen the effect on my body. I have great muscle tone. You can also try soy milk as well.

Vegetable Protein Pancakes
I Chapter use vegetable protein that is vanilla flavored. It is
the kind sold in drug stores and health food stores that are
meant to drink with milk. I make regular pancakes with
vegetable protein and eggs. About 65% of the mix is
pancake mix with about 35% Vegetable Protein mix. Then,
instead of milk, I use as eggs. I then use a grill that is
specifically designed to make pancakes. The presentation is
very important. Then I use sugar-free syrup. I make sure
there is enough syrup. If I need more to sell the goods, I
add some lower calorie whip cream or sprinkle on a few
chocolate chips. If the child likes bananas, then see if you
can get away with adding some of them to the mix.

Subsection 3 Exercise

Zombie Run Awesome Technology
You can get in shape by running from imaginary zombies.
https://itunes.apple.com/us/app/zombies-
run/id503519713?mt=8
https://play.google.com/store/apps/details?id=com.sixtostar
t.zombiesrunclient

Zombies, Run! 5k Training
You can exercise and run from imaginary zombies all at
some time.
https://itunes.apple.com/us/app/zombies-run!-5k-
training/id566596422
https://play.google.com/store/apps/details?id=com.sixtostar
t.zombies5ktraining

FItbit
Some people really love this to motivate them to exercise.
https://www.fitbit.com/

Pokémon GO
A lot of people have been very critical of this app.
However, if you have children that are gamers and are
inactive on a regular basis, this game can help get them
outside. Children with autism spectrum disorder sometimes
do very well with this game and can even get them to
socialize. If your child does not have these issues, then
maybe this is not for you.
http://www.pokemongo.com/

Chapter 5 Speech and Language Apps

There are a ton of apps for a speech and language pathologist to use with a student. The iPad is still king even though Chromebooks are being more commons within school systems. There are a number of apps to choose from.

AR/VR for autism
Artificial reality and virtual reality are currently being used to help students with autism.

Emotion Apps
Students can learn basic facial expressions with a number of different apps.

Social Skills App and Video
There are a number of online videos both paid and free that teach social skills for children of various ages and disabilities. There are also a number of highly rated apps that also teach social skills.

Early Intervention Apps
Finding an app for younger students that teaches language is an area of need. There are a number of apps that teaches the most basic language to younger students and/or students with a significant delay.

Everyday Language Apps
This category of apps has common objects that students can interact with and talk about.

Articulation Apps
Teaching articulation skills to students is something every speech and language pathologists does every day. This is a large category of apps that are often a good investment. There are several high-end articulation apps that teach the sounds and could be used often by a speech and language pathologist.

Assessment Apps
Testing a student's ability is an important aspect of being a speech and language pathologist. This category of apps has a number of very good options. Buying one higher-end app is a good investment.

Game Apps
Finding high-interest language apps is an area of need. There are a number of apps to teach articulation, listening skills, and other areas of language.

Abstract Language Apps
Teaching abstract language or language with very specific meaning and context is an area of need. There are a number of apps to teach specific areas of language.

Interactive Grammar Apps
Teaching a specific area of grammar is a part of the job that speech and language pathologist do. Having interactive examples of grammar are a big advantage to keeping activities higher interest.

Conversation and Sentence Apps

Being able to teach larger chunks of language is an important area for developing social langue skills. Written language requires languages skills composed of sentences. This makes conversation and sentence skills apps important.

Sound or Volume Apps

This app measures how loud someone talks. This app can also be used to measure other types of sounds. This can give feedback to students that lack self-awareness in this area. This could also be used with students that have hearing loss and cannot hear how loud or low they are talking.

Section 1 Autism Emotions

Understanding someone's emotions is something that should not be taken for granted. These apps give teachers multiple ways to represent the abstract concept of emotions. It also gives students a new way to communicate or express their answers. The approach will create more engagement by students.

ABA Flash Cards & Games - Emotions
This app has basic flashcards with pictures to represent emotions.
https://itunes.apple.com/us/app/aba-flash-cards-games-emotions/id446105144?mt=8

I Know How You Feel
This app teaches people about others emotional. The app gets very good ratings.
https://itunes.apple.com/us/app/i-know-how-you-feel/id960352272?mt=8&ign-mpt=uo%3D4

Avokiddo Emotions - Dress, Feed, Play With Animals
This app is designed for a speech and language pathologist with a sense of humor. You dress up silly animals and talk about their emotions. The app looks more like a game, but it gets very good ratings.
https://itunes.apple.com/us/app/avokiddo-emotions-dress-feed-play-with-animals/id661758013?mt=8

Let's Learn Emotions PRO
This is a highly rated app that teaches people about reading other people's emotions.
https://itunes.apple.com/us/app/lets-learn-emotions-pro-emotion-recognition-for-speech/id908762349?mt=8

Section 2 Robots and VR/AR for Autism

I strongly believe that in the future, we will see STEM, artificial intelligence, augmented reality, and virtual reality being used to help people with autism. A speech and language pathologist teaching social skills based on a script is not as compelling as virtual reality interacting with an autistic child. The fascination with technology and the predictable, repetitive nature can be a real advantage for a child with the disorder. When we are not good with an activity having an outlet to practice is needed. These technologies fill some of the void. When you lack speech skills, social skills, and an understanding of where to start having a dynamic outlet to practice is needed. There are already a number of examples out there. The technology to do much of this exists. We have to wait for people to figure out how to apply these technologies to develop new teaching and coping strategies.

Robots

Milo
This robot teaches children with autism social skills. If you watch some of the interactions in some of the online videos, it is heartwarming to observe.
https://robots4autism.com/

QTrobot
This is a robot designed to work with children with autism. The robot has different expressions and teaches social skills.
http://luxai.com/qtrobot-for-autism/

Augmented Reality

Empowered Brain by Brain Power
This is an augmented reality tool for autism. If you watch videos on this product, you will be amazed.
http://www.brain-power.com/autism/

Indiegogo
This product uses augmented reality to teach people with autism social skills. It is amazing.
https://www.indiegogo.com/projects/world-s-first-augmented-reality-glasses-for-autism#/

Virtual Reality

This amazing virtual reality tool teaches social and communication skills.
https://floreotech.com/
https://apps.apple.com/us/app/floreo-vr/id1160329033

Section 3 Social Skills Videos

Teaching social skills is a very important task. It is also a very difficult task. You have to express some very abstract and vital concepts to students that need to learn for everyday functioning. If you can use technology to give a dynamic way to display your concepts, then you have a very powerful tool to represent information. Students that use these apps have another way to practice self-expression and to test a new skill. Technology is often more engaging than role play or reading from a script.

Peers for Young Adults Honorable Mention
This website has a number of professional looking social skills videos for young adults.
http://www.routledgetextbooks.com/textbooks/9781138238718/videos.php

Popular Videos - Social skills & Autism
This is a playlist of a number of very good social skills videos.
https://www.youtube.com/watch?v=3RjRZ9jMfs0&list=PLQMoPKaeLDBwAj_k9bSFltGNo1XIQIv0t

Everyday Speech
This is a website with social skills videos.
https://everydayspeech.com/social-skills-videos/

Popular Videos - Social skills & School
A playlist for Social Skills
https://www.youtube.com/watch?v=NLm2BuW73m4&list=PLQMoPKaeLDBz3zwgZscsxmfxEo1swV0NX

Social Skills Videos YouTube Playlist
This playlist has a large number of social skills videos.
https://www.youtube.com/watch?v=Nd-bKUeP25s&list=PLmGvbTSYAlVk2zJ9u9X2GL_FaLxoj5daC&index=3

Popular Asperger's syndrome & Social skills videos YouTube Playlist
This playlist has a number of videos on social skills.
https://www.youtube.com/watch?v=IO378cKDmh0&list=PLxzCXFbagpJl3Gmi2pRTw-PYNkJkc-wly

4th Grade Social Skills
This website has a number of videos for younger children on the topic of social skills.
https://www.youtube.com/watch?v=H7w7yXkJTu0&list=PLr243_CfltVGGWIYigJi2QQfh7DjsnzpA&index=2

Social Skills Videos
This is a Pinterest account with a ton of links.
https://www.pinterest.com/cmcormier/social-skills-videos/

Discovery Education
Check to see if your school has a membership to Discovery Education. They have a number of videos on social skills and emotions in the health section. Good videos on social skills are hard to find.
http://www.discoveryeducation.com/

Free Videos for Autistic Kids
This website has a number of videos for children that have autism on a number of different topics.
http://www.freevideosforautistickids.com/social_skills.html

Section 4 Social Skills Apps

There are apps that allow you to create social skills content. It takes time to create content. As a professional teacher, I understand the amount of work that people do and creating all your lessons from scratch is a hard task.

There are apps that teach social skills. Even with many schools moving towards Chrome, the iPad is still king with special education. There are still a number of apps about social skills that are moderately priced and follow a theme or social skills curriculum.

Social Skills have grown as a big part of the curriculum often taught by speech and language pathologists. If you want to be a success, it is necessary to have good social skills to get along with others. The need to have friends is important for the young. As adults, there is a need to work with coworkers and others in the community; therefore, social skills are needed. Being part of a larger group is important to achieve higher social status.

Social Detective Honorable Mention
This app teaches social skills with videos.
https://itunes.apple.com/us/app/social-detective/id975189305?mt=8
There is also a book of the same name:
https://www.socialthinking.com/Products/You%20are%20a%20Social%20Detective
Website: http://www.socialskillbuilder.com/

226

Social Detective Intermediate
This is a very popular social skills curriculum and a highly rated app.
https://itunes.apple.com/US/app/id1079442478?mt=8

Social Detective Advance
If you like the series of apps, this is the next one to buy for students that have made progress. The app gets good ratings.
https://apps.apple.com/us/app/social-detective-advance/id1322321565

Let's be Social PRO: Social Skills Development
The app was made with input from SLPs. The app allows you to make original stories regarding social skills.
https://itunes.apple.com/us/app/lets-be-social!/id772244049?ls=1&mt=8
Website: http://www.myeverydayspeech.com/

10 Ways - a Social Skills Game
This is a social skills app and game.
https://itunes.apple.com/us/app/10-ways-a-social-skills-game/id1116372204?mt=8

Let's Learn Emotions PRO - Emotion Recognition for Speech Pathology & Special Education
This app helps to teach emotions.
https://itunes.apple.com/us/app/lets-learn-emotions-pro-emotion/id908762349?mt=8

Social Quest
This is a social skills app that gets some good ratings.
https://apps.apple.com/us/app/social-quest/id556089006?ign-mpt=uo%3D4

ConversationBuilder
The app teaches basic conversation skills.
https://itunes.apple.com/us/app/conversationbuilder/id4139
39366?mt=8

ConversationBuilderTeen
This app teaches conversation social skills to teens. I like
this app because we often think of social skills for younger
children and not teens.
https://itunes.apple.com/us/app/conversationbuilderteen/id5
51522479?mt=8

All About You All About Me Fun Deck
This app is designed to get a student to talk about different
situations. This app is good at teaching social skills or
starting a conversation app.
https://itunes.apple.com/us/app/all-about-you-all-about-
me/id449154858?mt=8
Website: http://www.superduperinc.com/products/view.asp
x?pid=MXAFD80#.Ud_zIG3ODIU

Social Stories Creator and Library for Preschool, Autism
and Special Needs
This app helps you create a story very quickly. This app is
used to teach social skills and basic conversations.
https://itunes.apple.com/us/app/social-stories-creator-
library/id588180598?mt=8&ls=1

Section 5 Early Intervention

The best time to address speech and language deficits is as early as possible. When a young child interacts with an app, the experience is highly engaging. For someone with very limited ability to express an idea, this gives a child a powerful tool. No one ever says, when a child has a problem. "we should have waited." In some cases, a student's verbal ability and ability to follow abstract directions and language can be so low that you need to start with an early intervention app. When picking an augmentative and alternative communication, there is often one need that sticks, out and that can dictate what you pick. If you work with Augmentative and Alternative Communication, you should see this as a resource for students.

My First AAC Honorable Mention
This app is designed for 18 months and older. It is designed to promote language with children that are in an early developmental stage. I like this app.
https://itunes.apple.com/us/app/my-first-aac-by-injini/id462678851?mt=8

SpeechStickers
This app gets young children to practice the basic sounds they need to learn. This is just an all-around a good idea for someone with a speech delay.
https://itunes.apple.com/us/app/speechstickers/id43610118 1?mt=8

Letter Muncher

This app teaches the basic sounds of letters to children learning to read.

https://itunes.apple.com/us/app/letter-muncher/id496956039?mt=8

Posco AAC

This is a simple but effective AAC app. It is designed for basic communication. Best of all, the cost is low. This app is good for young children or students with lower communication skills.

https://itunes.apple.com/us/app/posco-aac/id545435661?mt=8

Disfluency Index Counter

This is another good app by Smarty Ears. You can count correct words and syllables with this app. This app does a very good assessment at a reasonable price.

https://itunes.apple.com/us/app/disfluency-index-counter/id366359722?mt=8

Smarty Ears YouTube.com Channel:

http://www.youtube.com/user/SmartyEars

Section 6 Every-Day Language for Children

Often times, speech and language pathologists have a need to work on everyday language and common names. This is important for younger children. This can be done a number of ways. You can use pictures, worksheets, have a conversation, or use a device. Students usually do better with strong visuals that are interactive. There are a number of low-cost apps that show examples of everyday items that a student can interact with. This gives good visuals in the context that a person would see the items in the real world. The fact that you can engage the student in an interactive, hands-on activity makes this even better. I recommend that you consider the apps below for common language about common objects.

Sorting learning game for kids
This app has pictures of common objects, food, sporting equipment, and much more. A young child can sort related items and talk about them.
https://apps.apple.com/us/app/sorting-learning-game-for-kids/id501939025

Scene Speak
This app is designed to talk about a specific topic with a student.
https://itunes.apple.com/au/app/scene-speak/id420492342?mt=8

My PlayHome

With this app, you can teach common everyday language to young children. Think about it as an electronic doll house but much cooler. The fact that the app gets high ratings is a plus.

https://itunes.apple.com/us/app/my-playhome/id439628153?mt=8&ign-mpt=uo%3D4

My PlayHome School

This shows a number of common scenes within a school setting that you can talk about and interact with. The app also gets good ratings.

https://apps.apple.com/us/app/my-playhome-school/id922188121

Toca Life: Town

This app is an entire town that you interact with.

https://apps.apple.com/us/app/toca-life-town/id871694174

Draw and Tell

You can draw on a number of scenes and talk about what you are doing.

https://apps.apple.com/us/app/draw-and-tell/id504750621

Section 7 Learning Sounds for Young Children

Partners in Rhyme- Rhyming for Phonemic Awareness
With this app, you compare words based on pictures to decide if they rhyme.
https://apps.apple.com/us/app/partners-in-rhyme-rhyming-for-phonemic-awareness/id721334745

Touch the Sound
You have to figure out what pictures make a sound and then touch the picture to see for sure.
https://apps.apple.com/us/app/touch-the-sound/id506593890

SOUND BEGINNINGS
This app helps teach basic phonics and sounds.
https://apps.apple.com/us/app/sound-beginnings/id541898864

Sound Touch 2
You touch pictures to see what sound the picture makes.
https://apps.apple.com/us/app/sound-touch-2/id504519249
https://play.google.com/store/apps/details?id=com.soundtouch2&hl=en_US

Section 8 Apps with Free Versions

Having a section on free apps might not seem like a need or a proper category to some. As a teacher, I understand the difficulty of getting funds for very small purchases for education. The money is allocated from the top down. If you are on the ground floor, you do not have decision making power for small purchases. You have to ask administrators for even the most basic purchases. This is a mistake. If you go to a school for years, have to go to professional development on a regular basis and yet you cannot decide how ten dollars is spent. Teachers are so well known for buying their own supplies that it has been written in tax law. Companies that give away some basic free stuff win teachers over quickly. The truth is administrators will listen to teachers that can make a case. The process for buying items is longer than you would think. Lower level administrators have to go to their bosses to ask for money. If you use the free version of a product and love it, then you can make the case.

Lauren S. Enders, MA, CCC-SLP Honorable Mention
FREE Language Apps for SLPs
http://www.pinterest.com/lasenders/free-language-apps-for-slps/

Talking Tom Cat

A person talks to this app, and the app repeats what you said in a cartoon voice. The app is free. You can also buy a number of other similar apps for a few dollars from the app developer.

https://itunes.apple.com/us/app/talking-tom-cat/id377194688?mt=8

Here is a list of similar apps made by the developer. I have to warn you that some of the stuff in these apps is not appropriate for school. If you are a parent and you want to get one of these apps for your child that is okay. You want to be careful about teaching children inappropriate social behaviors. I used many of these apps with a family member, and I like them.

http://outfit7.com/our-work/

Verbally

If you are considering an AAC app, this is a good one to try first.

https://itunes.apple.com/us/app/verbally/id418671377?mt=8

Articulation Station

This is another popular app that is highly rated. Both the free and paid versions of Articulation Station are very good apps to help teach basic sounds to students.

https://itunes.apple.com/us/app/articulation-station/id467415882?mt=8

Section 9 SLP Assessments

The evolution of using iPads has not happened evenly. The apps in the area of speech and language have seen many apps appear. With the number of apps and the speed of this change, it is possible to go to two different speech and language pathologists and experience two very different approaches. A high-technology SLP could use any number of apps with an iPad that the traditional SLP would not. Both approaches are sound and good ways of working with peoples that have various issues.

Speech and language, educational or psychological tests have been scored on a computer for many years. However, doing an assessment on a mobile device is a huge advantage. An SLP could take a laptop with them to do an assessment.

What assessment to use and if they should be done with an iPad are a judgment call for a speech and language pathologists. The iPad is highly portable and is being used quite often by some speech and language pathologists. Some speech and language pathologists travel for their job. That would make many of these assessments more important.

Articulation Test Center Pro Honorable Mention
This app allows a speech and language pathologist to test students a number of different ways. This is a good way to assess what level a student is at.
https://itunes.apple.com/us/app/articulation-test-center-pro/id700440156?mt=8

Smarty Ears Apps
Many SLP have not yet moved to doing assessments with an iPad, but it is an interesting idea. A Speech and Language Pathologist that likes technology might want to check out some of the assessment apps from Smarty Ear apps.
http://smartyearsapps.com/

App names: Profile of Phonological Awareness, Sunny Articulation Phonology Test, Bilingual
Articulation Phonology Assessment, Dysphagia2Go, Disfluency Index Counter, Common Core Early Language Screener, AtEval2Go,
Videos for Smarty
Ears: http://www.youtube.com/user/SmartyEars?feature=watch

Articulation Assessment ToolKt
This app tests how well a child understands all the basic sounds. This app also gets good ratings.
https://itunes.apple.com/us/app/id371280343

Profile of Phonological Awareness (Pro-Pa)
This app tests phonological awareness.
https://itunes.apple.com/us/app/profile-phonological-awareness/id484657843?mt=8

Bilingual Articulation Phonology Assessment: English/Spanish
This app tests the phonological awareness for someone that speaks English and Spanish.
https://itunes.apple.com/us/app/bilingual-articulation-phonology/id460830225?mt=8

Section 10 Articulation/Teaching Sounds

Learning and pronouncing the sounds is a primary task that speech and language pathologist apps do. When asking a child to do a low-interest task, it is always helpful in creating high-interest activities. Trying to do something that you cannot do often ranks as a lower interest activity. When you cannot talk, it becomes harder to find people to talk to you and thus a downward cycle. That is why speech and language pathologists are so important. The amount of time and effort that it takes is considerable. If you are going to buy just a few apps and you are a speech and language pathologist I highly recommend looking at this section.

High-End Apps

Articulation Station Best of Class
This app teaches all the basic sounds that you need to learn. The app has a number of games and gets outstanding ratings. Do not be scared by the price. I used to think higher price apps were not worth it. This is an app that all speech and language pathologists can use often. If you are a decision maker in a school my advice, it buys this app. The good news is there is also a free version that you try first to build the case for a full purchase.
Free version that has in-app purchases:
https://itunes.apple.com/us/app/articulation-station/id467415882?mt=8
Full version
https://itunes.apple.com/us/app/articulation-station/id467415882?mt=8

See.Touch.Learn. Honorable Mention
I like this flashcard app for students with communication disorders, young children, and people learning to speak English. I like the way it is organized. They show you the pictures, and you have to guess what it is.
https://itunes.apple.com/us/app/see.touch.learn-pro/id467924373?mt=8

Word Vault Pro Honorable Mention
This is a free app with some in-app purchases. The paid version is a high-end teaching app for professional speech and language pathologists. The ratings for this app are outstanding. If you are a speech and language pathologist that likes using iPad app for therapy, this is a good option for teaching articulation. There is also a free version.
https://apps.apple.com/us/app/word-vault-pro/id672989436
https://apps.apple.com/us/app/word-vault-essential/id947222381

Articulation Station Español
If you are teaching articulation in Spanish here are two Spanish versions of Articulation Pro. One is free, and the other is a paid version.
https://apps.apple.com/us/app/articulation-station-pro-es/id1055553618
https://apps.apple.com/us/app/articulation-station-espa%C3%B1ol/id1055553611

Articulate it! Pro
This app teaches the sounds.
https://itunes.apple.com/us/app/articulate-it!/id391296844?mt=8

Speech Tutor Pro
This higher-end app teaches the sounds and articulations a number of different ways. This app is designed for professional speech and language pathologists.
https://apps.apple.com/us/app/speech-tutor-pro/id1323272450

Moderately Priced

Letter Muncher Honorable Mention
This app teaches the sounds of letters and vocabulary for young children. The app gets good ratings.
https://itunes.apple.com/us/app/letter-muncher/id496956039?mt=8&ign-mpt=uo%3D4

Pictello Honorable Mention
This is a simple way to create talking pictures. This app is good for a parent that wants to teach a child people's names and the names of common words or sayings. This app would also work well with a teacher or a Speech and Language Pathologist.
https://itunes.apple.com/us/app/pictello/id397858008?mt=8

Speech Journal
This app allows you to record your voice to pictures. It is made by the Mobile Education Store. The company makes a number of very good apps. This low-priced app is good to teach basic names to a student.
https://itunes.apple.com/us/app/speech-journal/id436945985?mt=8

Minimal Pairs Academy
This app teaches the 23 most common sounds. The app keeps track of data.
https://itunes.apple.com/us/app/minimal-pairs-academy/id483691470?mt=8

Articulation Scenes
The app teaches different sounds and also gets good ratings.
https://itunes.apple.com/us/app/articulation-scenes/id498857302?mt=8

SpeechStickers
This app is a moderately priced app that teaches basic sounds.
https://apps.apple.com/us/app/speechstickers/id436101181

The Sounding Out Machine - Assistive Reading Device
This app helps children sound out difficult words.
https://itunes.apple.com/us/app/the-sounding-out-machine-assistive-reading-device/id1063090009?mt=8&ign-mpt=uo%3D4

Multiple Choice Articulation
This app teaches students the different sounds. The ratings are also very good.
https://itunes.apple.com/us/app/multiple-choice-articulation/id580129419?mt=8

Missing Letter Articulation for Speech Therapy
The app does what the name says. It helps teach those sounds that some people struggle with.
https://itunes.apple.com/us/app/missing-letter-articulation/id961075823?mt=8

Multiple Choice Articulation
This app teaches the basic sounds and gets very good reviews.
https://itunes.apple.com/us/app/multiple-choice-articulation/id580129419?mt=8

Section 11 Articulation Games

Charades Articulation
Now, this is a fun way to teach language, and the good app gets good reviews.
https://itunes.apple.com/us/app/charades-articulation/id853990328?mt=8

Silly Sentence Articulation for Speech Therapy
This is a highly rated and fun app. It was developed for improving articulation.
https://itunes.apple.com/us/app/silly-sentence-articulation/id934544877?mt=8

Articulation Vacation
This is an articulation game app that gets very good ratings.
https://itunes.apple.com/us/app/articulation-vacation/id926324779?mt=8

Articulation Carnival Pro
This is a very good fun app.
https://itunes.apple.com/us/app/articulation-carnival-pro/id791572447?ls=1&mt=8

Dance Party Articulation
This is a fun way to teach articulation.
https://itunes.apple.com/us/app/dance-party-articulation/id1097737017

Articulation Games
This is a game app that teaches articulation.
https://itunes.apple.com/app/articulation-games/id561096403

Section 12 Language Games

Real Vocabulary Pro
The app has three games and even keeps score.
https://itunes.apple.com/us/app/real-vocabulary-pro/id825880776?ls=1&mt=8

Otsimo | Special Education ABA "Autism & Speech Therapy Games"
This app is a subscription service that teaches a number of basic skills to various special needs populations. According to the iTunes page, it is for learning disorders, attention deficit hyperactivity disorder, autism, and down syndrome." The app gets good ratings. The app has a number of games to choose from.
https://itunes.apple.com/us/app/otsimo-special-education-aba/id1084723774?mt=8

Secret Mission Articulation for Speech Therapy
You have to guess a word and you are given some of the letters. It is a game that forces you to practice the sounds.
https://itunes.apple.com/us/app/secret-mission-articulation/id822330124?mt=8

Mad Libs
The classic game turned app is always fun to play.
https://itunes.apple.com/us/app/mad-libs/id326885152?mt=8
https://play.google.com/store/apps/details?id=com.prh.mad libs_&hl=en
http://www.madlibs.com/apps/

10 Ways - a Social Skills Game
Jeopardy and many other games meet social skills with this app.
https://itunes.apple.com/us/app/10-ways-a-social-skills-game/id1116372204?mt=8

Fun English | Learn English
This app teaches English language skills to preschools up to about ten years of age. This app gets very good reviews. Students learn English by playing games.
https://apps.apple.com/us/app/fun-english-learn-english/id428920239

BluebeePals
These are animals that talk to you and tell a story along with an app on a tablet. You have to watch a video to get it. It looks like a lot of fun.
https://bluebeepals.com/products/

Jeopardy Labs
You can make your own Jeopardy game to study for a test.
https://jeopardylabs.com/

Jeopardy Rocks
You can build your own Jeopardy game with this website.
https://www.playfactile.com/

Language Adventures
This app teaches basic language in the form of a game. The game can help to engage students while teaching the basics sounds.
https://itunes.apple.com/us/app/language-adventures/id510822157?mt=8

Frog Game 2 - sounds for reading

This fun game app teaches the basic sounds needed for reading.

https://apps.apple.com/us/app/frog-game-2-sounds-for-reading/id924553338

Section 13 Listening Skills

Auditory Workout
This app is designed to help children with auditory processing disorders. The teaching tool is a high-interest basketball game. I like the app because it is research-based, and it is different from many of the speech and language apps that are available.
https://itunes.apple.com/app/auditory-workout/id518697520

Auditory Memory Ride
The description for iTunes says, "students aged six to 13 with central auditory processing disorder."
https://itunes.apple.com/us/app/auditory-memory-ride/id868209747

School of Multi-Step Directions
You get to learn about directions with a game in an app.
https://itunes.apple.com/us/app/school-multi-step-directions/id668209269

Hearbuilder
This is a listening game that works on sequencing, memory, direction, phonological awareness and keeps track of progress.
https://www.hearbuilder.com/

Section 14 Teaching Abstract Language

The best way to teach abstract concepts is with a multi-sensory approach. In many cases, abstract language can be better represented with pictures. If those pictures also have other interactive qualities that will create a higher level of engagement. If a child can touch the screen and can interact, then the child will have other means to express themselves through actions.

Category Therapy
Being able to put information in a category is an important part of any language. The concept is abstract and can be difficult to teach.
https://itunes.apple.com/us/app/category-therappy/id571551926?mt=8&ign-mpt=uo%3D4
Website: http://tactustherapy.com/apps/

Little Stories Pro
This app has short high-interest stories that teach a specific area of language. The app gets very good ratings.
https://itunes.apple.com/us/app/little-stories-pro/id1228283813?mt=8

Multiple Meanings Library
This app teaches multiple means. The English language has so much creativity that it is hard for some to grasp. The app is designed for speech and language pathologists, but I see it being useful for people that are learning English as a second language.
https://itunes.apple.com/app/multiple-meanings-library/id525605265

Conversation Therapy

This app is designed to teach higher-level expressive languages. The ability to have a conversation is difficult to teach.

https://itunes.apple.com/us/app/conversation-therappy/id620456076?mt=8

Company's YouTube.com

Channel: http://www.youtube.com/user/tactustherapy?feature=watch

Naming Therapy

This app teaches commonly used names in different contexts. The app has a lot of different ways to teach names. The app also tests the user.

https://itunes.apple.com/us/app/naming-therappy/id451093640?mt=8

Antonyms

This is a visual, game app that teaches antonyms.

https://itunes.apple.com/us/app/antonyms/id642104434?mt=8

Categories Learning Center

This app teaches the abstract concept of categories.

https://itunes.apple.com/us/app/categories-learning-center/id496646536?mt=8

RadSounds

This is a very cool app. The app teaches cause and effect with music and funny characters. It is so simple that it is what makes it brilliant.

https://itunes.apple.com/us/app/radsounds/id420977569?mt=8

Verbal Reasoning
This app challenges you to use abstract language.
https://itunes.apple.com/app/verbal-reasoning/id604097479

Section 15 Apraxia

Speech Therapy for Apraxia - Words
This app is designed for children with apraxia and other speech disorders.
https://itunes.apple.com/us/app/speech-therapy-for-apraxia/id586636734?mt=8&ign-mpt=uo%3D4

Apraxia Picture Sound Cards APSC
The app teaches words and sounds. You can keep track of your progress with data tracking. This is a well thought out app. The app has numerous pictures and sounds represented in it. The app is designed for a professional to use repeatedly with clients.
https://itunes.apple.com/us/app/apraxia-picture-sound-cards/id445165465?mt=8

Constant Therapy
This app helps individuals with apraxia and other speech and language issues.
https://apps.apple.com/us/app/constant-therapy/id575764424

Section 16 Interactive Grammar with iPad Apps

Teaching grammar is very important. When I teach writing to older students, I tell them to look up grammar on different websites. Even very good writers have a question of what to use. Getting in the habit of looking it up can help change old habits. The apps about grammar are really designed to use with one student. The apps I suggest are often used by a speech and language pathologist or sometimes a special education teacher. However, what do you do if you have one student that is behind in grammar in a large class? The issue with teaching a class with an app is the assessment. If you use a grammar app with the entire class, you have to figure out a way to do an assessment. No one wants to ignore how important it is to teach grammar. Teaching grammar when you are doing writing at the same time is difficult. These apps are fast ways to isolate specific areas of grammar and teach in an engaging way. It is also a good idea to project some of these apps to create a good visual for your students. The apps will give an interactive worksheet with multiple examples.

The Mobile Education Store Awesome Technology Maker
This app maker has a number of good apps about grammar.
http://mobile-educationstore.com/category/apps

TenseBuilder
This is another great app from the Mobile Education Store.
https://itunes.apple.com/us/app/tensebuilder/id427577382?mt=8

Rainbow Sentences
This app highlights the different parts of grammar with various colors.
https://itunes.apple.com/us/app/rainbow-sentences/id427578209?mt=8

Pronouns by Teach Speech Apps
This is a highly rated multi-sensory app that teaches pronouns.
https://itunes.apple.com/us/app/pronouns-by-teach-speech-apps/id965680245?mt=8

Questions2Learn
The app teaches how to respond to who, what, where, and when questions.
https://itunes.apple.com/us/app/questions2learn/id537209705?mt=8
Website: http://www.speechpups.com/

Action Words
This app teaches verbs to young children. It shows simple pictures of the action.
https://itunes.apple.com/us/app/action-words/id511783094?mt=8

StoryBuilder for iPad
You can create a story with this app. The app asks you questions, and you give answers to create your story.
https://itunes.apple.com/us/app/storybuilder-for-ipad/id377631532?mt=8

Section 17 Conversation and Sentences

An important area of helping students improve on is a conversation and the structure of language. Speech and language pathologists spend hours on articulation and social skills; this is sometimes a lost finer point. We often take for granted our ability to phase information correctly on demand. This skill does not come as naturally to some as others. Working on this skill sets the stage for social skills, conversations, and articulation mistakes. If you like using an iPad as part of your practice, I recommend looking here for apps.

Picture the Sentence HD
This app is used to teach basic receptive and expressive language. This is a highly rated app.
https://itunes.apple.com/us/app/picture-the-sentence-hd/id478599625?mt=8
This company has other good apps in this category:
http://hamaguchiapps.com/

SentenceBuilderTeen
This is the teen version of the popular app.
https://itunes.apple.com/us/app/sentencebuilderteen/id465018367?mt=8

ConversationBuilderTeen
It is harder to find apps to teach language to teens.
https://itunes.apple.com/us/app/conversationbuilderteen/id551522479?mt=8

ConversationBuilder

This app helps students work on basic conversational sentences in social situations.

https://itunes.apple.com/us/app/conversationbuilder/id4139 39366?mt=8

ConversationBuilderDeluxe

https://itunes.apple.com/us/app/conversationbuilderdeluxe/i d467903946

Sentence Builder

The application focuses on building sentences around a picture. The application allows students to practice using proper connecting words. The application has three different challenging levels.

https://itunes.apple.com/us/app/sentencebuilder-for-ipad/id364197515?mt=8

Sentence Maker

This app makes creating sentences an interactive game. This app is for young children making short, simple sentences.

https://itunes.apple.com/us/app/sentence-maker/id499150658?mt=8

Section 18 Vocabulary

Vocabulary is an important area that everyone can improve on. Having enough words is an issue. Correctly using the words, we have is another issue. If you use the wrong word, the looks you get will give you an awkward feeling. Being able to describe something can make or break a story. The power that words have means getting peeople's attention and the power get them to work with you. To be a leader, you must be able to utilize the powers of words and part of that is context and vocabulary. Even if you want to blend in the background, it is important to have words to get what you need, want, or otherwise desire. That means vocabulary development.

Language Adventures
This app teaches basic language in the form of a game. The game can help to engage students while teaching the basic sounds.
https://itunes.apple.com/us/app/language-adventures/id510822157?mt=8

Real Vocabulary Pro
This is a comprehensive app with a number of strategies to teach vocabulary. The ratings are also very good.
https://itunes.apple.com/us/app/real-vocabulary-pro/id825880776

Section 19 Measure Sound Volume

The volume we speak at is something we take for granted. Most of us have the self-awareness to the point we can talk at a level that people will not hear across the room. Anyone could speak too loudly. For some with autism or speech disorders, this can be a real issue. One way to teach this is with feedback. That does not mean you just scold someone. With these simple apps, you can give a quantitative number that illustrates just how loud they are. Then a student can practice talking lower and see the difference based on a measured number.

iPhone/iPad

Decibel X - dBA Noise Meter
This is a very good free sound meter.
https://itunes.apple.com/us/app/decibel-x-dba-noise-meter/id448155923?mt=8

Decibel X PRO: dBA Noise Meter
This is a paid version of a good sound meter app.
https://apps.apple.com/us/app/decibel-x-pro-dba-noise-meter/id1257651611

Decibel : dB sound level meter
This is an inexpensive sound meter with some very good reviews. You can also make some in-app purchases.
https://apps.apple.com/us/app/decibel-db-sound-level-meter/id1227650795

Voice Meter Pro

This is a sound meter that you have to pay a small fee to buy. However, the app is very good and worth the money if you use it on a regular basis.

https://apps.apple.com/us/app/voice-meter-pro/id686934049

Google Play Apps

Sound Meter dB

This is a very good sound meter from the Google Play Store.

https://play.google.com/store/apps/details?id=com.gamebasic.decibel&hl=en

Sound Meter - Decibel meter & Noise meter

This is a sound meter app that gets some good reviews.

https://play.google.com/store/apps/details?id=app.tools.soundmeter.decibel.noisedetector&hl=en_US

Chapter 6 Augmentative and Alternative Communication

Communication devices are a very important tool for someone with significant communication difficulties. Most people buy the same communication app for all of their students with communication disorders. A communication device is something a person with a communication disorder has to carry everywhere. The same individual does not have the power to request the app or device that best suits their needs. It is important to know that there are choices. That does not mean we have to pick a different app for each student. Peace of mind is about knowing you have options when making difficult life-altering choices. Please be aware that some apps have specific qualities that might be right for students with specific needs.

AAC App or Augmentative and Alternative Communication Apps
These are apps that transform a tablet, computer, or smartphone into a communication device.

High-End Augmentative and Alternative Communication Apps
These are the higher priced major augmentative and alternative communication apps that are most commonly used.

Lower-End Augmentative and Alternative Communication Apps

There are a number of free or inexpensive augmentative and alternative communication apps. Typically, these apps are used to test if an augmentative and alternative communication app would work with a student before making the investment.

Augmentative and Alternative Communication or AAC Text-Based Communication Apps

These are communication apps that allow a student to type what they want to say, and then the device engages in verbal communication. Think of this as augmentative and alternative communication apps without pictures or symbols. There are several high-end apps in this category.

Dynavox

This is the name of a company. Dynavox is known for being good at mounting communication devices for people with physical disabilities and for being able to use software where you can control the device with your eyes.

Foreign Language Augmentative and Alternative Communication Apps

These are augmentative and alternative communication apps for people that communicate in languages other than English. There are several made by major AAC brands.

Section 1 AAC - Augmentative and Alternative Communication Apps

Many people know about big-name augmentative and alternative communication. There are more choices than one would think. Often times people pick the same app. If you like a communication app, and that is your comfort zone, there is nothing wrong with that. Often students present unique situations and challenges. Finding an app that meets an important need for a student with a communication disorder is important. At no time do I feel satisfied that I know everything on this subject. If you find it important to pick the right app, it is important to consider and eliminate lessor apps. It is also important to know why you decided on an app and then test out your hypothesis by trying the app with a student.

Touch Chat HD Honorable Mention
This is another high-end AAC app. This app is often recommended by professionals in the field. You can buy several add-ons with more vocabulary that adds to the cost. They are known for having the best vocabulary. This app is good for someone with a higher vocabulary that would like a large number of terms. The best apps in the category tend to be the ones that are the most user-friendly. That is because of the time commitment adding pictures and vocabulary.
https://itunes.apple.com/us/app/touchchat-hd-aac/id398860728?mt=8
Website: http://www.silver-kite.com/touchChat

Proloquo2go Honorable Mention
This was the first high-end AAC app. It allows someone to communicate by typing words and clicking on pictures. https://itunes.apple.com/us/app/proloquo2go/id308368164?mt=8

LAMP Words For Life
This is a high-end AAC app. The price is higher than many of the other high-end apps out there. The app has a good number of pictures for someone that is younger, that is learning to communicate. It is more of a picture-based app. For children or some people with a limited vocabulary having more pictures is an advantage. https://itunes.apple.com/us/app/lamp-words-for-life/id551215116?mt=8
Website: http://aacapps.com/lamp/

Avaz for Autism
It is the best app in this class. It is very user-friendly. I highly recommend this app.
Website: http://www.avazapp.com/
https://itunes.apple.com/us/app/avaz-for-autism/id558161781?mt=8
Spanish version
https://itunes.apple.com/us/app/avaz-espanol-aac-app-para/id923997149?mt=8
Google
Play https://play.google.com/store/apps/details?id=com.avazapp.autism.en.avaz&hl=en

TalkTablet NEO

This app costs slightly less than the higher-end apps but looks similar to many of them. You can adjust the app to allow four tiles to limit choices for younger children or those with a limited vocabulary. The app also has a number of pictures as well. You can buy this app on a number of platforms.

https://apps.apple.com/us/app/talktablet-pro-autism-aphasia/id1436382584

Windows https://www.microsoft.com/en-us/store/apps/talktablet-aac-speech/9nblggh337bk

Google

Play https://play.google.com/store/apps/details?id=com.gus inc.talktableta

Speak for Yourself

This is a highly rated, high-end AAC app.

https://itunes.apple.com/us/app/speak-for-yourself/id482508198?mt=8

aacorn AAC

This is a highly rated, high-end AAC app.

Website: http://www.aacornapp.com/#solution

iPad: https://itunes.apple.com/us/app/aacorn/id732419715?mt=8

Verbally Premium

This high-end communication app gets very good ratings.

https://itunes.apple.com/us/app/verbally-premium/id470081134?mt=8&ign-mpt=uo%3D4

Section 2 Dynavox

For a long time, I did not include Dynavox in my books. Purchasing an iPad is generally less expensive than buying a similar product from Dynavox. I included Dynavox because there still are solid reasons to buy the various products that Dynavox offers. You can even buy an iPad from the Tobii Dynavox website with a case. The case gives the feel of the higher-end communication devices. The price of many of the Tobii Dynavox products has gotten much lower over the years. For people with disabilities, the Tobii Dynavox products have some real advantages that cannot be ignored. The Tobii brand is known for eye-tracking for people with physical disabilities. An individual with a severe physical disability can use a Dynavox commination device by moving their eyes. Tobii does make software that you can use to control a computer by moving the mouse with your eyes for gamers as well. The Dynavox communication devices are known for having mounts that will fit a wheelchair. As a result, individuals with physical disabilities, the Tobii Dynavox is a consideration. Fitting a mount sounds like a simple task but often is much harder than you think. No one wants to order a needed device and have to return it, start over again, and order another product. If you are an expert, what you recommend is expected to work and be a good product. The truth is assistive technology specialist have to know so much that we cannot know everything. If you work with the physically disabled, please consider Tobii Dynavox as a viable option.
https://www.tobiidynavox.com/en-US/

ConnectIT Mounting Plate for Speech Case 9.7" or 12.9"
https://www.tobiidynavox.com/en-US/accessories/mounts/connectit-mounting-plate-speech-case/

Speech Case without iPad
https://www.tobiidynavox.com/en-US/devices/multi-access-devices/speech-case/

Accessories
https://www.tobiidynavox.com/en-US/products/accessories/

Tobii Eye Tracking Products
You can buy an eye tracking mouse with many of the communication devices that are sold on this website. If you scroll down on the webpage, you will see some of the eye tracking products.
https://www.tobiidynavox.com/en-us/products/devices/

Section 3 AAC Text-Based Communication High End

Text Based Augmentative and Alternative Communication (AAC) apps have you type what you want to say. This is not a new type of app. However, more apps are being made with this theme. As a result, it gets a separate section.

Predictable
This is a high-end text-based communication app with good ratings. The app works with switches.
https://itunes.apple.com/us/app/predictable/id404445007?mt=8
https://play.google.com/store/apps/details?id=com.tbox.predictable_4&hl=en_US

Proloquo4Text
This is a very highly rated, high-end, text-based communication app.
https://itunes.apple.com/us/app/proloquo4text-text-based-aac/id751646884?mt=8

Text to Speech!
This is an iPad/iPhone app that says whatever you type. This is simply free and get the job done. The reviews are also pretty good.
https://itunes.apple.com/us/app/text-to-speech/id712104788

Verbally
This app has a good rating. You have to type what you are going to say. The app has a free version that gives you a better idea if you want this app.
https://itunes.apple.com/us/app/verbally-premium/id470081134?mt=8

Section 4 Accessories

You might ask yourself why is there a category with only one item in it? The answer is that I am hoping to fill out more items in this category in the future. If I don't this one item is so important that I will break my rule of having multiple items to establish a category. One of the things I see is when a student uses an augmentative and alternative communication is they hold the device up as if the words are coming from the device. Having a speaker that is attached to the individual is a powerful statement. Telling a student, the words come from them is wonderful but getting them to believe it is something else. An attached speaker is a great way to convey this. I think this should be standard in the future. The device that is used will get smaller. We will see the day in our lifetimes where a person that is unable to talk without a device and uses a device will not visually stand out in a crowd quite the same way. I image a device that fits in your pocket. It can be activated with your eyes or hands. The best part is people will hear the sounds and see the person and not the device.

Tokk Smart Assistant
This is a speaker that clips onto you. Individuals with a speech disorder often hold up a device when talking. With this speaker, the words sound like they are coming from you because the words are coming from you.
https://tokktech.com/product/tokk-smart-speaker-black/

Section 5 Low-End AAC Apps

School systems are top town organization when it comes to purchases. The process of buying something with a purchase order is long and less fun, then you think. Governments are designed to prevent people from stealing money and instilling accountability. This is not helpful when you want to buy something vital for ten dollars. The process of buying something is so annoying that some business refuses to work with governments. The businesses that do work with governments create more problems. If you do not pay your bills in thirty days many businesses with rightly full cut off your credit. Governments always pay up eventually.

This debacle creates the need for free stuff and makes it profitable. In order for a teacher to buy a five-dollar app, they need to say I used the app, and it is totally awesome. So educational technology businesses that shows up to conferences and gives free samples often times create interest. Teachers are cheap partly because of the complicated process called a purchase order and an unwilling to rock the boat. Those of us that lead the field are often diplomatic more than being rebels. If I can try a product and see the benefit, then I can lobby my boss, and they can lobby their boss. That person can go to the business department and ask to pay the bill.

This creates the need for apps and products that teachers do not mind buying on their own with the hope of trading up for something better. A low-cost app that can make the argument for a higher priced app is an important stepping stone to where you need to go.

iPad Apps

Choiceworks
This is a very simple AAC app. It helps students with a basic schedule or common events.
https://itunes.apple.com/us/app/choiceworks/id486210964?mt=8

EESpeech Basic - AAC Communication Notebook
This is an organizational app as well as one for basic communication.
https://itunes.apple.com/us/app/eespeech-basic-aac-communication/id833923960?mt=8

See Me Talk
A special education teacher made this app by taking feedback from an SLP and parents. The interface is simple and has a basic vocabulary.
https://itunes.apple.com/us/app/see-me-talk/id590399460?mt=8

Oxford Picture Dictionary, Second Edition
Picture dictionaries define words with pictures. This type of dictionary is designed for someone with limited communications skills. It is a great idea that is not used enough.
https://itunes.apple.com/us/app/oxford-picture-dictionary/id591484885?mt=8&ign-mpt=uo%3D4

Chrome AAC Apps

Picto4me AAC Communication Boards
https://chrome.google.com/webstore/detail/picto4me-aac-communicatio/hdckhnghilfajdimkkfhfejcihcdlgdl

Google Play Apps Low-End AAC

CommBoards - Communication Assistant – AAC
This app is designed for basic communications for students that have autism. The app gets some very impressive reviews.
https://play.google.com/store/apps/details?id=com.shmoontz.commboards

AAC Autism myVoiceCommunicator
This is an AAC app.
https://play.google.com/store/apps/details?id=apphouse.software.autismspeaks&hl=en

Niki Talk
This is an AAC app with a different interface.
https://play.google.com/store/apps/details?id=it.alessandrolarocca.nikitalk
Website: http://www.nikitalk.com/Buy.aspx

LetMeTalk
The app allows basic communication.
https://play.google.com/store/apps/details?id=de.appnotize.letmetalk

Aac Talking Tabs
The app has pictures and words to help you communicate.
https://play.google.com/store/apps/details?id=it.ac19.aac

Section 6 AAC Apps with Foreign Languages

The United States of America is a multilanguage country. There is no official language of the USA. With the influx of immigration in the past few decades and no stop in sight, we have to assume that some children with autism and other serious communication problems will speak languages other than English. This complex immigration problem is happening in many of the other industrialized nations. This challenge is real, and as an educator, my job is not to judge or engage in politics. My job is to help everyone and anyone that is a child or teen that I work with.

Proloquo2go Honorable Mention
This was the first high-end AAC app. It allows someone to communicate by typing words and clicking on pictures. The app has add-ons for French and Spanish.
https://itunes.apple.com/us/app/proloquo2go/id308368164?mt=8
http://www.assistiveware.com/support/faq/page/10

Touch Chat HD Honorable Mention
This is another high-end AAC app. The app has add-ons that are in Spanish. Touch Chat also has add-ons for English that are for bilingual students. They are known for having the best vocabulary. This app is good for someone with a higher vocabulary that would like a large number of terms.
https://itunes.apple.com/us/app/touchchat-hd-aac/id398860728?mt=8
Website: http://www.silver-kite.com/touchChat

MyTalkTools Mobile
This is a highly rated AAC app. The app does a good job
with visuals. You can also buy packs in different
languages.
https://itunes.apple.com/us/app/mytalktools-mobile/id324286288?mt=8&ign-mpt=uo%3D4
Google Play
https://play.google.com/store/apps/details?id=com.MTA.MyTalkMobile&hl=en
Website:
http://www.mytalktools.com/dnn/2/Products.aspx

Predictable Português
If you were looking for an AAC app that is for Portuguese,
you now have an option.
https://itunes.apple.com/us/app/predictable-portugu%C3%AAs/id941528690

Avaz en Français
This is an AAC app for some that speeches French.
https://apps.apple.com/fr/app/id937115434

Chapter 7 Physical Disabilities

Section 1 State Agencies for Disabilities

Every state has a state agency or more than one that displays assistive technology and or loans the technology to schools or individuals. This is a valuable resource. No one can know everything about technology to help people with every type of disability and subsection of disability. If a state agency has a loan program look at the database and sees what they have. This is a great way to see what is out there in terms of technology that others are using.

Pass It On Center
If you want to find assistive technology state organizations that can showcase technology, answer questions, provide services, or loan a device, this is the link for you. If you scroll down, you have the option of picking the state and type of disability. This is an excellent search tool.
http://passitoncenter.org/reuse_locations.php

The National Equipment Exchange Depot
Search databases of technology nationwide. This will help you access a ton of information and ideas.
http://need-at.org/needat/index.php

AssitiveTech.net
This is a list of state links to assistive technology agencies from all around the United States of America.
http://assistivetech.net/webresources/stateTechActProjects.php

Section 2 Assistive Technology in Operating Systems and Browsers

One of the best places to find assistive technology or UDL technology is for free in your operating system. Big name brands have figured out there are a lot of people that need this technology and that number will only grow with an aging population, a greater understanding of the technology, and a greater social acceptance of using this type of technology.

Chrome

Android Accessibility Suite
https://play.google.com/store/apps/details?id=com.google.android.marvin.talkback&hl=en_US

Get started on Android with TalkBack
https://support.google.com/accessibility/android/answer/6283677?hl=en

You have to use the Chrome browser to see this information.
Chrome Web Store - Accessibility - chrome.google.com
https://chrome.google.com/webstore/category/ext/22-accessibility

Turn on Chromebook accessibility features
https://support.google.com/chromebook/answer/177893?hl=en%3Futm_source%3Demail

Google Accessibility
Google has a number of very popular products. This link
will give you all of them and the accessibility features you
need.
https://www.google.com/accessibility/products-
features.html

Grackle
This company makes several products to make Google
Suite products more accessible.
https://www.grackledocs.com/pricing-grackle-suite-2/
Grackle Accessibility Checker for G Suite
https://chrome.google.com/webstore/detail/grackle-
accessibility-che/copojmaamcpblldileiipebpfjahcnjf?hl=en

Chrome Accessibility
https://chrome.google.com/webstore/category/collection/ac
cessibility

Windows

Windows 7
https://www.microsoft.com/enable/products/windows7/
Windows 7 Accessibility Tutorials
https://www.microsoft.com/enable/training/windows7/

Windows 8
https://www.microsoft.com/enable/products/windows8/

Windows 10
https://www.microsoft.com/enable/products/windows10/

Microsoft Accessibility
https://msdn.microsoft.com/en-
us/windows/uwp/accessibility/accessibility

Mac

Accessibility Apple
This link has considerable information on accessibility for
Apple products.
https://www.apple.com/accessibility/

Mac Accessibility
http://www.apple.com/accessibility/osx/

Accessibility iOS
https://www.apple.com/accessibility/iphone/

Apple Watch
http://www.apple.com/accessibility/watch/

Firefox

Firefox is one of the most popular browsers. It has a ton of
free accessibility features that you can use.
https://support.mozilla.org/en-US/kb/accessibility-features-
firefox-make-firefox-and-we

Section 3 Mice Handheld

I am asked for solutions for mobility issues from time to time. When the mobility gets significantly worse, one consideration is a mouse that is controlled with your eyes. There are a number of solutions before you get to that point. The problem is none of them seem perfect. It is painful to watch someone struggling in this area, especially if it gets worse over time. That fact that you can use a joystick for a computer or tablet is a better answer in some cases. The problem is there is no answer that is going to make you feel great. We all want to make it better. The truth is hindsight is 20/20. You only know after you use it. Even amazing assistive technology specialist cannot see the future. I often hear the line that "I want the perfect device for this child." This is a popular line. That is why many states have programs that demonstrate technology or lone it to you. All vendors have return policies. There are a ton of options, and anyone can predict the best option each time should play Lotto. I suggest playing the devil's advocate and just being very good at what you do and always expect better.

Joystick

n-ABLER Pro Joystick (PC)
This mouse is easy to move the courser with a joystick.
https://www.enablemart.com/n-abler-pro-joystick

J-Pad Bluetooth Joystick for iPad
You can control your iPad with this joystick mouse. It also
has two buttons to help you perform different functions.
https://www.enablemart.com/j-pad-bluetooth-joystick-for-ipad

Two Companies to look at:

http://www.infogrip.com/

http://www.pretorianuk.com/mouse-alternatives

Section 4 Mice Head/Eye

Tobii
This company has mice that are controlled by your eyes.
They sell a range of products. The less expensive mice are
marketed for gamers, and the more expensive are for
assistive technology. Once you put something on the
market, for one thing, it is hard to stop people from using
for a slightly different purpose. If the lower cost product
does the job, then go with it.
http://www.tobii.com/

Camera Mouse
This is a free downloadable program that allows you to
move your mouse with a webcam. You move your head,
and the mouse moves. You stare at a link, and it clicks on
it.
http://www.cameramouse.org/index.html

Gazespeaker
This is free software for Windows products that allows you
to control a computer or tablet with your eyes. You need to
buy hardware to get this software to work.
http://www.gazespeaker.org/
This link gives a great list of devices that you can use with
the free software. The webpage also gives some excellent
examples of other possible options as well. There is a lot of
good information here.
http://www.gazespeaker.org/devices/

Glassouse

This device allows you to control your computer, tablet, or other electronic devices. It is glasses that control the cursor on a computer, and you can bite down to click. This is designed for people with significant disability.

http://glassouse.com/

Section 5 Physical Disability

VGo Honorable Mention
If a child cannot physically attend school because of a chronic illness, this robot is a very good option. The robot is controlled via a device. The robot moves just like a student would. You can see and hear as if you are there. The student can talk to other students or teachers. The robot looks like something out of a science fiction movie. However, it works, is real and a great way to educate students with any number of issues.
http://www.vgocom.com/

iPhone Voice Control
You can use your iPhone by talking to it. This is a big advantage for people with physical limitations.
https://support.apple.com/guide/iphone/use-voice-control-instead-of-siri--iph3c511340/ios

Panther Math paper
This app is designed for someone that cannot write. It is a math app.
https://itunes.apple.com/us/app/panther-math-paper/id547090551?mt=8

Axs Map
This website gives ratings and information on wheelchair assessable locations.
http://www.axsmap.com/

tecla

This app gives individuals with physical disabilities more options with how to control an iPad or iPhone.

https://gettecla.com/

https://itunes.apple.com/ca/app/tecla/id1317772309?mt=8

https://play.google.com/store/apps/details?id=com.gettecla.e&hl=en

iPad Pro Stands

This product is a stand for your iPad. You can have your iPad hands free in front of you. The stand will also let you use an iPad as a document camera. If you want your iPad on display next to you, this is a great product.

https://ipaddocumentcamera.com/pages/ipad-pro-stand

Section 6 iPad Cases

I usually only look in two places when searching for a case for an iPad. One place I look at is Lauren Enders' Pinterest account, and the other is Amazon.com. Amazon takes purchase orders from schools, and that helps.

Lauren S. Enders, MA, CCC-SLP Honorable Mention
Lauren has an awesome Pinterest board. I have great respect for people in the field that share information that can help others.
http://www.pinterest.com/lasenders/

Big Grips
This is a very popular case for students with a disability. The cases are reasonably priced.
http://www.biggrips.com/frame.html

iKBC CD108BT Wired + Wireless 2 in 1 Mechanical Keyboard with Cherry MX Brown Switch for iOS, Android, Windows and Mac (Bluetooth 3.0, PBT OEM Profile Keycaps, 108-Key, Navy Blue Color, ANSI/US)
Mechanical keyboards are a high-quality keyboard. This is a full keyboard, including the number pad. This keyboard can be paired with different devices. The keyboard works with iOS, Android, and Windows. You can use this keyboard with many different devices.
https://www.amazon.com/CD108BT-Wireless-Mechanical-Keyboard-Bluetooth/dp/B07F61DNJP/ref=sr_1_5?keywords=full+keyboard+ios&qid=1549742483&s=gateway&sr=8-5

MoKo Wireless Bluetooth Keyboard, Ultra-Thin Foldable
Rechargeable Keyboard for iPhone, iPad 9.7, iPad Pro, Fire
HD 10, Compatible with All iOS, Android and Windows
Tablets Smartphones Devices, Gray
This keyboard is portable, reasonably priced, and has a
good design. The keyboard is on a slight angle for comfort.
The compact design is excellent for travel.
https://www.amazon.com/MoKo-Ultra-Thin-Rechargeable-
Compatible-
Smartphones/dp/B07BNB6R7G/ref=sr_1_6?keywords=full
+keyboard+ios&qid=1549742483&s=gateway&sr=8-6

DICTOPRO D100 Wireless Bluetooth Keyboard Universal
for Portable Tablets Smartphones iOS Windows Android
Multi-Device Folding Small Ultra-Slim, Best Built-in
Battery, Compact & Powerful Blue Tooth
This keyboard is compact and sells for a reasonable price
https://www.amazon.com/Bluetooth-Universal-
Smartphones-Multi-Device-Ultra-
Slim/dp/B072X931BP/ref=sr_1_1?keywords=keyboard+io
s&qid=1549743050&s=gateway&sr=8-1

CHESONA Bluetooth Keyboard Ultra Slim Sliding Stand
Universal Wireless Bluetooth Keyboard Compatible Apple
iOS iPad Pro Mini Air iPhone, Android Galaxy Tab
Smartphones, Windows PC
This is a good keyboard that does not fold at a reasonable
price.
https://www.amazon.com/s?k=keyboard+ios&s=review-
rank&qid=1549743043&ref=sr_st_review-rank

VicTsing Ultra-Slim Portable Bluetooth Keyboard,
Wireless Keyboard for iOS (iPhone, iPad), Android,
Windows, Mac Computer, Laptop, Tablet, Smartphone,
and Other Bluetooth Enabled Devices, Silver
This is a very good keyboard for a great price.
https://www.amazon.com/VicTsing-Ultra-Slim-Portable-
Bluetooth-
Smartphone/dp/B07M6SW6SS/ref=sr_1_9?keywords=key
board+case+ios&qid=1549743302&s=gateway&sr=8-9

iPad Keyboard Case for iPad 2018 (6th Gen) - iPad 2017
(5th Gen) - iPad Pro 9.7 - iPad Air 2 & 1 - Thin & Light -
360 Rotatable - Wireless/BT - Backlit 10 Color - iPad Case
with Keyboard
This is a high-quality keyboard-case.
https://www.amazon.com/iPad-Keyboard-Case-2018-
6th/dp/B07H42YGLR/ref=sr_1_3?keywords=keyboard+ca
se+ios&qid=1549743409&s=gateway&sr=8-3

Section 7 Voice Controlled Devices

Technology for people with physical disabilities is a growing area. With an aging population and people without a disability wanting smart devices, the demand for certain devices is increasing. When you have a market and the technology is within reach only good things can happen. Over time we will see smart technology activated by your voice doing any number of tasks.

Voice-activated devices are an amazing technology that can help a number of people. For people with physical disabilities being able to control your home with your voice is a real need. If you cannot type activated voice devices are a great way to surf the internet. Voice-activated devices can be used with students that have a number of other disabilities. Many of these devices can answer important questions for a student. Some examples are how to spell words or add numbers. Many of these devices will set a timer, tell you your schedule, or set voice reminders. As we become a more connected world, the uses for these devices will increase to fill even more needs.

Google Home
Technology is going to voice. The day will come that you will talk to your home or a device and everything will happen. For most people, this is way cool. For people with physical disabilities that is life-changing. Converting a home into a smart home for someone with a disability for a reasonable price is in reach.
https://store.google.com/us/product/google_home?hl=en-US

HomeKit
This product is made by Apple. You can control various aspects of your home with Siri.
https://www.apple.com/ios/home/

Echo
You can control a number of items in your home with this voice controlled device. This is a developing technology that in time, will allow for voice control of more items in your home.
https://www.amazon.com/all-new-amazon-echo-speaker-with-wifi-alexa-dark-charcoal/dp/B06XCM9LJ4

Echo Dot
The Dot is less expensive than the Echo but does most of the same features.
https://www.amazon.com/All-new-Echo-Dot-3rd-Gen/dp/B0792KTHKJ

Section 7 Switches and Other Devices

Jane Farrel Honorable Mention
Jane Farrell Gives you a list of apps the work with switches. Reading this list works better than trial and error. It also gives you examples of apps that you can suggest to clients with mobility issues.
http://www.janefarrall.com/switch-accessible-apps-for-ipadiphone-non-aac/

Lauren S. Enders Honorable Mention
This is a list of apps that works with switches.
https://www.pinterest.com/lasenders/switch-accessible-apps-and-ipad-compatible-switch-/?lp=true

TetraMouse
This company makes computer mice for people with physical limitations.
http://tetramouse.com/

AirBar
You can turn your laptop screen into a touch-screen with AirBar.
http://www.air.bar/

Xbox Adaptive Controller
This adaptive controller was featured in a Superbowl commercial. This is an adaptive controller for individuals with physical disabilities. People with disabilities should enjoy video games just like everyone else.
https://www.ablenetinc.com/resources/xbox/

Game Box Controllers
This link goes to video game controllers that are for people with physical disabilities. People don't think about the many things people with physical limitations go through. For some people, using your hands for repetitive motion can be a form of exercise.
http://www.rjcooper.com/game-controller/index.html

Page Flip
Page Flip is hardware. You turn pages on an iPad iBooks with your feet. Musicians can turn pages without using their hands. It also works for the physically disabled. The pedals work with any app that accepts Bluetooth. So, if you can use a keyboard, you can use pedals.
Company: http://www.pageflip.com/

Tecla Switch
This is a large button that can be touched to manipulate an iPad. This is an option for the physically disabled person that wants to use an iPad or another mobile device. On the website, I could not find a price.
Website: https://gettecla.com/collections/switches

AT Tools for Computer Access
Some great information from Lauren S. Enders Pinterest account
http://www.pinterest.com/lasenders/at-tools-for-computer-access/

Learn How to Add a Switch

This video shows you how to add a switch or a Bluetooth device.
http://atmakers.org/2016/10/ios-switch-control-on-a-budget-using-bluetooth-kbd/

Use Switch with iPhone, iPad, or iPod touch
https://support.apple.com/en-us/HT201370

Switch Access for Android
https://support.google.com/accessibility/android/answer/6122836?hl=en

Games that work with a switch

If you are looking for games for someone with a physical disability that will work with a switch:
https://www.helpkidzlearn.com/#
http://www.shinylearning.co.uk/freegames/

Use a Smartphone/Tablet without Touching

AssistiveTouch
The iPad has a number of features for individuals with assistive technology. If you are looking for more options for an individual with a disability, then this is worth a look.
https://support.apple.com/en-us/HT202658

Sesame Phone
This is a smartphone that you do not touch. The video on this phone is awesome!
https://play.google.com/store/apps/details?id=com.sesame.phone_nougat&hl=en
Website: http://sesame-enable.com/phone/

Tecla Access
With this app, you can control your device with a switch or other hardware.
https://play.google.com/store/apps/details?id=ca.idi.tekla

Google TalkBack
This app is for people with low vision that need an alternative way to communicate with their device.
https://play.google.com/store/apps/details?id=com.google.android.marvin.talkback

Chapter 8 Deaf & Hearing Impaired

Section 1 Deaf & Hearing Impaired

P3 Mobile
P3 a mobile app for VRS (Video Relay Service). The app gets outstanding ratings. This helps people that are deaf take phone calls. The app gets very good ratings.
https://itunes.apple.com/us/app/p3-mobile/id432523572?mt=8
https://play.google.com/store/apps/details?id=us.purple.purplevrs
Mac
Purple P3 https://itunes.apple.com/us/app/purple-p3/id1057351582?mt=12

Purple VRI
This is a video interpretation service for the hearing impaired. This is called Video Remote Interpreting. (VRI)
https://itunes.apple.com/us/app/purple-vri/id479694412?mt=8
https://play.google.com/store/apps/details?id=us.purple.purplevri&hl=en
https://signlanguage.com/vri/

Motion Savvy
This company makes tablets that you sign to, and then it talks. Someone that only knows sign language and can't talk can now communicate. This technology is totally awesome.
http://www.motionsavvy.com/

Signing Savvy ASL Sign Language Video Dictionary
This is a webpage where you type in a phrase, and it gives you the visual for the ALS sign.
https://www.signingsavvy.com/sign/TRANSLATE/5810/1

Sign Language Dictionary
https://www.spreadthesign.com/us/

ASL Sign Language Translation
This site is good if you want to learn common signs to communicate.
http://www.handspeak.com/translate/

Right Hear
This is for a school or business that wants to be more accessible to people with visual disabilities. You install devices around the area that you want to make more accessible. With the app, a visually impaired person gets vital information about the location there are at. They can include obstacles. The app speaks to them about valuable information on their environment.
https://right-hear.com/
https://itunes.apple.com/us/app/righthear/id1061791840
https://play.google.com/store/apps/details?id=com.righthea
r

Section 2 Closed Captions

Web Captioner Best of Class
This website does free captioning and uses large text. If you need captioning done on the fly, this is the best place to look. This is an absolute hidden gem.
https://webcaptioner.com/

Google Documents Voice Typing with an iPad as a Microphone Honorable Mention
If the text is not big enough, I recommend using Google Documents Voice Typing. If you use an iPad as a microphone and project what you are saying on a whiteboard, it does the same thing as Google Slides Closed Captions. Except the type is much bigger. The larger text is needed in many cases.
https://support.google.com/docs/answer/4492226?hl=en

Google Slides Closed Captions Honorable Mention
With this feature, an educator can talk, and each word that is stated is displayed on your projector. To have a free way to display every word you say is very valuable for students with any kind of hearing impairment.
https://support.google.com/docs/answer/9109474?hl=en

Closed Captions Apple TV
You can find information on how closed captions work on Apple TV here.
https://support.apple.com/guide/tv/activate-subtitles-and-captioning-atvb5ca42eb9/tvos

Closed Caption Windows 10

This is information on the closed caption settings for Windows 10.

https://support.microsoft.com/en-us/help/21055/windows-10-closed-caption-settings

YouTube

You can add closed captions to YouTube videos.

https://support.google.com/youtube/answer/2734796?hl=en

PowerPoint Closed Captions

This gives you information on how to add closed captions to PowerPoint videos.

https://support.office.com/en-us/article/add-closed-captions-or-subtitles-in-powerpoint-df091537-fb22-4507-898f-2358ddc0df18

Closed Captions Creator

This is a program that adds closed captions to videos. There are several paid versions to choose from.

https://www.closedcaptioncreator.com/

Section 3 iPad Apps Deaf & Hearing Impaired

iOS TTY Calling
Answer or make TTY calls from your iPhone
https://support.apple.com/en-us/HT207033
New in iOS 10: Software TTY
Calling http://ow.ly/tWje306BRhh

Dectone Hearing aid
This app amplifies and adjusts sounds to help people with
hearing difficulty.
https://itunes.apple.com/gb/app/dectone-hearing-
aid/id1356112754?mt=8

Hearing Helper
This app has speech to text that can translate to different
languages. The app if for people that are hearing impaired,
deaf, and/or speech a different language.
https://itunes.apple.com/us/app/hearing-
helper/id1391454121?mt=8

ASL Translator
You can translate English words into American Sign
Language. The app gets very good ratings. Just remember
that translations are not exact.
https://itunes.apple.com/us/app/asl-
translator/id421784745?mt=8&ign-mpt=uo%3D4

ASL Fingerspell American Sign Language Dictionary
This app shows you all of the letters in American Sign
Language.
https://itunes.apple.com/us/app/asl-fingerspell-american-
sign-language-dictionary/id1110489445?mt=8

ASL: Fingerspelling (Lifeprint.com)
This app teaches you the American Sign Language Alphabet.
https://itunes.apple.com/us/app/asl-fingerspelling-lifeprint-com/id605558017?mt=8&ign-mpt=uo%3D4

Signed Stories
These are children's stories that you can read but are also told with sign language.
https://itunes.apple.com/us/app/signed-stories/id550966811?mt=8

ASL Dictionary from NTID
This is an American Sign Language dictionary.
https://itunes.apple.com/us/app/asl-dictionary-from-ntid/id510152499?mt=8

Sign Me A Story
This app teaches sign language with by telling a story. I love the concept! Based on the ratings, I am not the only one.
https://itunes.apple.com/us/app/sign-me-a-story/id628136371?mt=8&ign-mpt=uo%3D4

ASL Dictionary American Sign Language
This is an American Sign Language dictionary.
https://itunes.apple.com/us/app/asl-dictionary-american-sign-language/id902008714?mt=12

Section 4 Google Play Deaf & Hearing Impaired

Live Transcribe
This is a speech to text app that is designed for someone that is deaf or hard of hearing. You talk, and it turns your words to text.
https://play.google.com/store/apps/details?id=com.google.audio.hearing.visualization.accessibility.scribe&hl=en_GB

BuzzCards
This app helps a deaf person communicate with someone that does not know sign language.
https://play.google.com/store/apps/details?id=com.sorenson.buzzcards

Hand Talk Translator Brazilian Sign Language (Libras)
The app translates written words or spoken language into Brazilian Sign Language (Libras).
https://play.google.com/store/apps/details?id=br.com.handtalk&hl=en

Hearing Test
This app gives a basic hearing test. It can be used to illustrate a point. If you truly want to measure hearing I would recommend going to a professional for testing.
https://play.google.com/store/apps/details?id=mobile.eaudiologia

BuzzStickers

These are sign language stickers. They are better described as sign language emojis. With this, app texting just got better for the deaf.

https://play.google.com/store/apps/details?id=mvrs.sorenson.com.buzzstickers

ntouch

This app allows you to communicate with a sign language interpreter.

https://play.google.com/store/apps/details?id=com.sorenson.mvrs.android

ASL Dictionary

This app is a dictionary for sign language.

https://play.google.com/store/apps/details?id=com.signtel

DeafNote Free

This is a note-taking application.

https://play.google.com/store/apps/details?id=tashuapps.deafnote

Chapter 9 Visual Impairment

There are a number of technologies that can be used for someone with a visual impairment.

Artificial Intelligence
This is software or hardware that can make decisions that was typically only done by humans in the past. An example might be recognizing faces.

Braille
These are bumps on paper or dots on a computer screen that represents letters for a person with a visual impairment.

Take a Picture Ask a Question Apps
These are apps that a person with a visual impairment can use to have a sighted individual describe an object for them.

GPS Apps
These are apps that will tell you your locations, describe your surroundings, and give you directions of how to find something.

Reverse Projecting or Projecting onto an iPad or Computer
Typical when you project something it is a computer projected onto a screen. When you want to do the same exact thing onto a device, I use the term reverse projecting. This can be done to project a document onto a device for someone with a visual impairment to see.

Magnifiers
This is hardware and/or software that enlarges text on the fly.

Section 1 Visual Impairment

American Foundation of the Blind
The website has a catalog of technology for the visually impaired. If you look for technology for someone with a visual impairment, bookmark this website.
http://www.afb.org/prodBrowseCategory.aspx

Perkins Library Honorable Mention
This website has services for people with visual impairments. There are numbers of items to choose from. The library has audio books and Braille.
https://www.perkins.org/library/services

Qiat.org
This is a PDF guide to using assistive technology with the visually impaired.
https://qiat.org/docs/resourcebank/TEBO_VI_Resource_Gu ide.pdf

Google TalkBack
This app is for people with low vision that need an alternative way to communicate with their device.
https://play.google.com/store/apps/details?id=com.google.a ndroid.marvin.talkback

Light Detector
This app can detect light. It notifies you of the presence of light by making a sound. The brighter the light, the louder the sound gets.
https://itunes.apple.com/US/app/id420929143?mt=8&ign- mpt=uo%3D4

HeyTell

This app is the voice version of text messaging. Just think about all that typing you are doing that could be avoided with this app.

https://itunes.apple.com/us/app/heytell/id352791835?mt=8
https://play.google.com/store/apps/details?id=com.heytell
https://www.microsoft.com/en-us/store/p/heytell/9wzdncrfj3hn?rtc=1
Website and video: http://heytell.com/front.html

Talkler - Email for your Ears

This app will read your email out loud.

https://itunes.apple.com/us/app/talkler-email-for-your-ears/id570741489?mt=8

Section 2 Artificial Intelligence

Seeing AI: Talking Camera for the Blind Honorable Mention
This free app gives someone with low vision information about their surroundings. The app also reads text to you. The app gets excellent reviews.
https://itunes.apple.com/us/app/seeing-ai-talking-camera-for-the-blind/id999062298?mt=8
https://www.microsoft.com/en-us/seeing-ai/

Envision AI
This app can read text from an object and give you a description of a scene.
https://itunes.apple.com/us/app/envision-ai/id1268632314?mt=8
https://play.google.com/store/apps/details?id=com.letsenvision.envisionai&hl=en_US

VocalEyes AI
This very highly rated app uses artificial intelligence to help the visually impaired better understand their environment.
https://itunes.apple.com/us/app/vocaleyes-ai/id1260344127?mt=8

Eye-D
This app recognizes objects, reads print text, tells you where you are, and what is around you. This app does a number of things.
https://itunes.apple.com/us/app/eye-d/id1354363634

Section 3 Braille

BARD Mobile
This app can give someone with a visual impairment access to braille and talking books. The app is used with a service from the National Library Service.
https://itunes.apple.com/us/app/bard-mobile/id705229586?mt=8
Google
Play https://play.google.com/store/apps/details?id=gov.loc.nls.dtb&hl=en
Amazon Appstore http://www.amazon.com/Library-of-Congress-BARD-Mobile/dp/B016760320/ref=sr_1_1?s=mobile-apps&ie=UTF8&qid=1458957724&sr=1-1&keywords=bard

Orbit Reader
This device help translates text into Braille. You can use a Mini-USB cord or an SD card to connect to the text.
http://www.aph.org/orbit-reader-20/

MBraille
This app allows you to write your everyday tasks using Braille.
https://itunes.apple.com/us/app/mbraille/id639199558?mt=8&ign-mpt=uo%3D4
Braille Tutor
This app helps you learn Braille.
https://itunes.apple.com/us/app/braille-tutor/id1082934024?mt=8

Section 4 Hardware for the Visually Impaired

eSight
The eSight headset looks like it is straight out of a science fiction movie. A camera picks up what you are looking at. Mini-viewers are inside the device. You can then adjust the picture to help see it better. The picture can be enlarged. The price is on the higher-end side. However, this technology does what other devices cannot. The opportunities that can be created as a result are tremendous. I love the concept. This could be the future for the visually impaired.
https://www.esighteyewear.com/

OrCam MyEye 2
You wear this item on glasses and it tells you information on different visuals. OrCam can read text be programmed to recognize faces, products, read barcodes, read money, and tell you the color of items. This is an amazing technology.
https://www.orcam.com/en/myeye2/

MyReader 2
This is similar to OrCam MyEye 2. This is a scaled down model.
https://www.orcam.com/en/myreader2/

Enchroma

These glasses make colors come out like never before. It can be used with individuals that are color blind to allow them to see more vivid images. There are a number of videos of people reacting to using these glasses online. You would have to try these glasses to understand how they work.

https://enchroma.com/

These websites have handheld video magnifiers.
https://www.magnifyingaids.com/Portable_Video_Magnifier
http://www.freedomscientific.com/products/lowvision/
https://www.maxiaids.com/t/video-magnifiers
https://irie-at.com/low-vision/handheld-video-magnifiers/
https://shop.magnifyingamerica.com/Hand-Held-Magnifiers_c3.htm
http://www.beyondsight.com/index-shopping.php

Section 5 Take Picture Ask Question Apps

Be My Eyes – Helping blind see
This app allows a visually impaired person to show a
person with normal vision an object. Then ask what it is?
iPad: https://itunes.apple.com/us/app/be-my-eyes-helping-
blind-see/id905177575?mt=8
https://play.google.com/store/apps/details?id=com.bemyey
es.bemyeyes
Website: http://www.bemyeyes.org/

BeSpecular - Help The Blind
A visually impaired person takes a picture and then asks a
question of someone with the app. This can solve the
everyday questions that visually impaired people have.
https://itunes.apple.com/us/app/bespecular-help-the-
blind/id1068947453?mt=8

TapTapSee
This app helps someone with a visual impairment figure
out what object they are looking at.
https://itunes.apple.com/us/app/taptapsee-blind-visually-
impaired/id567635020?mt=8

Aira – Visual Info On Demand
This service is a combination of using technology and
people to help low vision individuals identify objects and
solve problems.
https://apps.apple.com/us/app/aira/id1071584352?ign-
mpt=uo%3D8

Section 6 GPS Apps

Nearby Explorer
This app uses GPS and helps you navigate independently without the help of another person. The app gets good reviews.
https://apps.apple.com/us/app/nearby-explorer/id1095698497

Nearby Explorer Online
You can find your location with this free app. The same company makes a similar paid app called "Nearby Explorer."
https://apps.apple.com/us/app/nearby-explorer-online/id1095699328

Ariadne GPS
This is a talking map program with GPS. A person with a visual impairment could use this to direct them to different areas. The app is listed on several websites and is widely recommended.
https://itunes.apple.com/US/app/id441063072?mt=8&ign-mpt=uo%3D4

Sunu Band
This is a band that looks like a watch that warns you of what is around you. It uses echo location to give you feedback on what is around you.
http://www.sunu.io/

BlindSquare

This is a GPS app developed for the blind. The app tells you about information regarding your surroundings. This app works regardless of how you are traveling.

https://itunes.apple.com/us/app/blindsquare/id500557255?mt=8

Section 7 Projecting a Computer on an iPad

When someone has a visual impairment often times, they cannot see the board. Today's classrooms have a projector. What these apps do is project the computer the teacher is using on the iPad or computer that the students are using. The student can then hold the device in a position that makes it easier to view. These apps need WiFi to work. This is also called reverse projecting.

join.me Awesome Technology Author's Pick Honorable Mention
This app allows you to project a computer onto an iPad or computer. It is web-based. The free version allows you to do this with a small group of 10. The paid app allows up to a group of 250. Instead of projecting onto a board, you can project your computer onto multiple iPads.
https://itunes.apple.com/us/app/join-me/id409811927?mt=8
Website: https://join.me/
https://play.google.com/store/apps/details?id=com.logmein.joinme&hl=en\
join.me for Google Calendar
https://chrome.google.com/webstore/detail/joinme-for-google-calenda/nemahdoihakfniciobefoebllhlobdok?hl=en-US

Mirroring360
This is mirroring software. There is a one-time charge if you decide to buy it.
https://www.mirroring360.com/

Conference Pad

This app allows you to project the same screen onto multiple devices.

https://itunes.apple.com/ca/app/conference-pad/id377782792?mt=8

Section 8 Document Cameras

I feel like document cameras that project wirelessly are a hidden secret. There are document cameras that can project to computers or tablets. If a teacher needs to enlarge text, they can in real time. You put a document under the wireless document camera, and it projects onto a device. The student can enlarge and manipulate the text in real time. This can make the enlarging of text easy. Once you set up the device, there is little or no planning to enlarge worksheets. The cameras are affordable and can be used for regular education students if the student with a disability moves, refuses to use it or graduates. The upside of this is large, and the downside is small.

iZiggiHD Honorable Mention
This is a wireless camera that will project onto an iPad.
https://www.ipevo.com/prods/Ziggi-HD_Plus_USB_Document_Camera

IPEVO Whiteboard
This app is used with a document camera made by IPEVO. The document camera displays a picture of the document then you mark up the document with the whiteboard app.
https://itunes.apple.com/us/app/ipevo-whiteboard/id594766738?mt=8
https://play.google.com/store/apps/details?id=com.ipevo.whiteboard&hl=en
https://chrome.google.com/webstore/detail/ipevo-whiteboard/ngabidjikmpanokhnajohenclgjedjkp?hl=en-US

HoverCam Honorable Mention

HoverCam makes document cameras that are of very good quality. The reason I list them is that you can connect the document camera to a device every way possible. That includes wirelessly to an iPad. This is very helpful if you want to project directly onto an iPad to help someone with a visual impairment. Projecting to an iPad is a great way to keep a student's attention. They have several document cameras that have these awesome features. I recommend looking at them and picking the one that fits your needs best.

http://www.thehovercam.com/

VZ-X Wireless, HDMI & USB 8MP Document Camera - Ipevo
https://www.ipevo.com/prods/VZ-X_Wireless_HDMI_USB_8MP_Document_Camera

Section 9 Magnifiers

Background on Electronic Magnifiers

People with low vision use different types of magnifiers in order to see print text, pictures, and other objects. Apps on tablets are a less expensive than hardware solutions. Most people carry around a smartphone. With a magnifier app, they don't have to carry a bulky and expensive device. The magnifier apps make it easier for people with milder vision problems to have a device that enlarges text.

Software and Hardware

ZoomText
This is a PC software program for people that have a visual disability. The program does just about everything. It is as if someone sat in a room and thought of every possible way to allow an individual to see the text better.
http://www.zoomtext.com/

iPad Pro
The size of the iPad Pro, high resolution, and the ability to do work with the iPad Pro just cannot be ignored. It can also be held up to your face, and it has the ability to enlarge text with the accessibility features
http://www.apple.com/ipad-pro/

iPad Apps

SuperVision+ Magnifier
This is a magnifier for someone that really needs to see fine detail up close.
https://itunes.apple.com/us/app/supervision+-magnifier/id691435681?mt=8

Over 40 Magnifier and Flashlight
You can magnify an object. It lights up the center of interest. It can even freeze on one frame to make it easier to read.
https://itunes.apple.com/us/app/over-40-magnifier-flashlight/id381663967?mt=8

Magnifying Glass With Light - digital magnifier with flashlight
You can magnify and sharpen the text with this app.
https://itunes.apple.com/us/app/magnifying-glass-light-digital/id406048120

BigMagnify Free
This is a highly rated magnifying app.
https://itunes.apple.com/us/app/bigmagnify-free-zooming-magnifier/id393247466?mt=8

Magnifier - Flashlight Zoom
This magnifier app gets some great ratings.
https://itunes.apple.com/us/app/magnifier-flashlight-zoom/id1208906051?mt=

Google Play Magnifiers and Visual Impairment

Magnifier Pro
This is a highly rated app.
https://play.google.com/store/apps/details?id=com.app2u.magnifierpro&hl=en

Magnifying Glass Flashlight
This is a very highly rated magnifying app.
https://play.google.com/store/apps/details?id=com.Mbase_Utilities.MagnifierFlashlight

Magnifying Glass Flashlight PRO
This is a magnifying app that gets excellent ratings.
https://play.google.com/store/apps/details?id=com.magnifyingglass.flashlightpro

Magnifier
This is a highly rated and popular app that magnifies text.
https://play.google.com/store/apps/details?id=app.melon.magnifier

Magnifying Glass + Flashlight
This is a magnifier and light all in one.
https://play.google.com/store/apps/details?id=com.rvappstudios.magnifyingglass

Cozy Magnifier & Microscope +
This app has a high rating.
https://play.google.com/store/apps/details?id=com.hantor.CozyMagPlus

Magnifier

This is a magnifying app.

https://play.google.com/store/apps/details?id=mmapps.mobile.magnifier

Seeing Assistant Magnifier

This is a magnifier that helps you adjust color and contrast to see better.

https://apps.apple.com/us/app/seeing-assistant-magnifier/id692742390

Section 10 Calculators

Big Calculator Low Vision
This is a calculator for someone with low vision.
https://itunes.apple.com/us/app/big-calculator-low-vision/id1177115993?mt=8

Talking Scientific Calculator
This is a talking calculator that has a number of higher-level functions.
https://apps.apple.com/us/app/talking-scientific-calculator/id411433609

Talking Calculator
The calculator has big buttons, and it talks to you. It is very good for the visually impaired and has benefits for many other students that need things read to them.
https://itunes.apple.com/us/app/talking-calculator/id424464284?mt=8

Chapter 10 Projects

One of the biggest barriers to learning is a lack of engagement. We live in a world where everyone can look up information instantaneously. Video games and move much faster. Kings and queens of the past did not have all these amazing technologies. This change in our society affects education. Attention spans are getting shorter, and academic expectations is getting higher. As a field, education must use technology to engage students. When students get instant feedback from dynamic computer tools, that leads to engagement. Right now, the distractions educators face is often technology driven. Mobile phones, earbuds, games on demand, and YouTube videos unrelated to content areas can take away from instruction. Many of these distractions are a teacher's job to notice and stop during class. To remove barriers, I recommend using engaging hands-on projects with technology. I have collected a list of the best technology to engage this generation.

Presentation
This means using tools like Slides or PowerPoint. If you are creative, there are a number of other online tools that can make creating a presentation dynamic.

Video
We live in a world where most people have a video camera in their pocket. There are a number of great options to create videos for educational purposes.

Podcast

This is when you record audio and post the recording on the internet for others to gain information from. This is a very powerful tool. There are a number of tools on various platforms to make this happen.

Green Screen

These are screen of one color that can be taken out when you make a video. The background is then replaced by a picture or a video. Green Screen by Do Ink is one of my favorite tools. Green Screen by Do Ink is an iPad app that is user-friendly.

Screen Recorder

There are a number of programs that will record your computer screen. This is a great way for a student to comment on a subject. There are free options and even screen recorders that will record a webcam on top of the screen. The technology is much easier to use, then one would think. This is a great option for projects.

Hyperdocuments or HyperDocs

This is when a number of links to documents, webpages, and resources are put into a word processing document. This is typically done with Google Documents. Hence the "documents" or "Docs" in the word. This is a dynamic way to engage students in the learning process.

Interactive Whiteboards

This is when you use an app, software program, or a website as a whiteboard. There are a number of programs with many tools. If you record a video of yourself using the whiteboard that makes this tool far more interesting. If students record themselves explaining a concept or a project with an interactive whiteboard, then the tool becomes extremely useful. Virtual Reality

This has to be the coolest technology that is currently emerging. Google Expeditions and other tools are exciting to use. If you use one of the higher end virtual reality headsets, it is like having an Imax threader on your head. Over time people will figure out how to finetune this tool for educational purposes.

Publishing
There are several great tools to create a book or publish writing. Students can also publish art as part of the book they create. Publishing a book is rewarding. This is a great way to show real-world examples.

Curation Tools
There are a number of tools to collect and display different types of information that can be found electronically. Some of these tools are adapted for use in the classroom. This can be a great way to do research, have students collaborate, or share information with students. The various tools are also very user-friendly.

Section 1 Presentations

Pear Deck Honorable Mention
This is an interactive presentation program. You can ask students questions in real time and control what the students see on their device. The program has many more interactive features. Pear Deck can be used for free and has premium features that can be used for a monthly fee. You should visit the website to understand what the product offers.
https://www.peardeck.com/

Padlet Honorable Mention
You can create a presentation, planning, collaborate, or gather information with this blank canvas. You can add video, pictures, and text.
https://padlet.com/
https://itunes.apple.com/us/app/padlet/id834618886?ls=1&mt=8
https://play.google.com/store/apps/details?id=com.wallwisher.Padlet

Prezi Honorable Mention
This is a very popular presentation website, and it has a lot to like. You can insert a video picture or text. You also don't have to go in order like a traditional presentation.
https://prezi.com/

PowToon (Website)
You create an animation and a voice-over. The outcome is something very cool. Some people might call this a video, but it has the simplicity of a presentation. This is a website you should look at if you want to do something different and interesting.
http://www.powtoon.com/

PowToon Presentations Edu (Chrome)
This creates fun animations that can be used to create a presentation.
https://chrome.google.com/webstore/detail/powtoon-presentations-edu/ogodblbnhpbcmcjcoopbalconhnloagl?utm_source=chrome-ntp-icon

Glogster
Glogster has some similarities to Prezi. It is a very good presentation website. You might want to go to their education website when you Google them.
http://edu.glogster.com/

Haiku Deck
You can create some interesting presentations with Haiku Deck.
https://itunes.apple.com/us/app/haiku-deck-presentation-slideshow/id536328724?mt=8&ign-mpt=uo%3D4
Chrome: https://chrome.google.com/webstore/detail/haiku-deck/mipkilokfhepolbekmdghlclfnpfpief?hl=en

Animoto: Slideshow Maker
You can make a great presentation with this app. The reviews are outstanding.
https://apps.apple.com/us/app/animoto-slideshow-maker/id459248037

Stick Around by Tony Vincent & Explain
Everything Awesome Technology Hidden Gem
With this app, you can make an interactive game or
presentation. This app is so different I not sure what
category to put it in. This app is for a techie teacher that
does a project with students. This is an awesome app.
https://itunes.apple.com/us/app/stick-around-by-tony-vincent/id557949353?mt=8
A ton of great resources on their website:
http://learninginhand.com/stickaround
Video: https://vimeo.com/86032409

Info Graphics
These are graphics you create to explain a concept or tell a
story. This graphic can involve pictures and words. It is an
interesting concept to integrate into a project with your
students.
http://elearninginfographics.com/
http://www.schrockguide.net/infographics-as-an-assessment.html

Section 2 Video

Adobe Spark Video, Animated Videos in
minutes Honorable Mention
This is a highly rated video editing app/website. Schools
can get the premium version free. That includes a control
panel that the technology leadership in the district can use.
https://spark.adobe.com/edu/
https://itunes.apple.com/app/id852555131

Flipgrid Honorable Mention
Flipgrid allows users to collect a group of videos on a
subject. You ask a question and have different people
across the globe answer the question or within the
classroom. Students can each make a video on a subject
then have the class watch each video. Parents can record a
video from a smartphone, tablet, or computer to be part of
the class. Flipgrid is so simple yet powerful that it is just
hard to ignore. The concept is simple and innovative at the
same time.
https://info.flipgrid.com/

YouTube Editor
You can edit a video with YouTube. The question is, "do
you want a class to post on YouTube?" That would work
for some situations and not others. You can make videos
private. That means only people invited to use a video can
see them. YouTube.com video editor is still one of the very
best free online video editors.
https://www.youtube.com/editor
Information about private videos:
https://support.google.com/youtube/answer/157177?hl=en

Animoto Video Slideshow Maker
You can add pictures and videos to make an awesome presentation.
https://itunes.apple.com/us/app/animoto-video-slideshow-maker/id459248037?mt=8&ign-mpt=uo%3D4
https://play.google.com/store/apps/details?id=com.animoto.android.videoslideshow&hl=en
https://chrome.google.com/webstore/detail/animoto-video-maker/cambaldalpopjjmpfogbpikpbhembepl
Animoto gives awesome deals to educators. It is a good idea to look into this for your classroom.
Website: https://animoto.com/education/classroom
Animoto Video Maker
You can add pictures and videos to make an awesome presentation.
https://chrome.google.com/webstore/detail/animoto-video-maker/cambaldalpopjjmpfogbpikpbhembepl
Animoto gives good deals to educators. It is a good idea to look into this for your classroom.
Website: https://animoto.com/education/classroom

Magisto Video Editor & Movie Maker
This is a very highly rated video editing app.
https://www.magisto.com/
https://itunes.apple.com/us/app/magisto-video-editor-movie-maker/id486781045?mt=8

Shadow Puppet Edu
This app is designed for younger students. They make a very simple and interesting video. The app gets good reviews.
https://apps.apple.com/us/app/shadow-puppet-edu/id888504640

Biteable
With this website, you can make a video presentation. The application is very user-friendly.
https://biteable.com/

Sway
This website makes it easy to take pictures and then tell a story. Sway is user-friendly and effective.
https://sway.com/
https://www.microsoft.com/en-us/store/p/sway/9wzdncrd2g0j

Section 3 Podcasts

Anchor Honorable Mention
This is a very popular and highly rated podcast creation tool.
https://anchor.fm/
https://itunes.apple.com/app/apple-store/id1056182234?mt=8
https://play.google.com/store/apps/details?id=fm.anchor.android&referrer=utm_source%3DAnchor%2520Home%26utm_medium%3Dcpc%26utm_campaign%3DAnchor%2520Home%26anid%3Dadmob

Voice Record Pro Author's Pick
This is a very good free app that will record your voice and then allows you to email it or transfer through other means.
https://itunes.apple.com/us/app/voice-record-pro/id546983235?mt=8

Smart Record - Voice Recorder & Transcribe Audio
This app will record your voice, and if you pay extra will give you a transcript. This is a good idea if you have a meeting that could use a transcript for various reasons.
https://itunes.apple.com/us/app/smart-record-voice-recorder/id1008197697?mt=8

Voice recorder
This is a voice recording app with a good rating.
https://play.google.com/store/apps/details?id=com.app.studio.voicerecord&hl=en

Smart Voice Recorder
This is a very popular recording app.
https://play.google.com/store/apps/details?id=com.andrwq.recorder

Voice Recorder
This is a free online voice recorder.
http://online-voice-recorder.com/

Soundation
This is a free online sound studio.
https://soundation.com/

Recorder Plus Editor
You can record audio and make edits with this app
https://itunes.apple.com/us/app/recorder-plus-editor/id502271511?mt=8

Section 4 Green Screens

Green Screen by Do Ink Best of Class
This is a simple and very popular green screen app.
https://itunes.apple.com/us/app/green-screen-by-do-ink/id730091131?mt=8

Touchcast Honorable Mention
This video recording and editing app is amazing. You can use the app with or without a green screen. The amount of simple yet brilliant effects are transformative. You can turn out a basic video with some cool effects rapidly. The app has features that you would expect to see in a higher-end software program. The amount of amazing feature is truly awesome.
https://www.touchcast.com/
https://itunes.apple.com/us/app/touchcast-studio-present-with-smart-video/id603258418?mt=8

There are many ways to make a green screen. You can hang a large curtain, paint a wall green, or use a large sheet of plywood. In a library where the masses gather, it is a good idea to have a green screen that is aesthetically pleasing. You probably do not want walls that do not match or a sheet of plywood. To get started you might want to try an inexpensive King-sized sheet. If this is something that becomes a popular part of the library, then you should strongly consider a green curtain or backdrop.

LimoStudio Photo Video Photography Studio 9x13ft Green Fabricated Chromakey Backdrop Background Screen, AGG1855
This is a large curtain that you can hang in your library.
https://www.amazon.com/LimoStudio-Photography-Fabricated-Chromakey-Background/dp/B00QJIGHA4/ref=pd_lpo_421_tr_t_3?_encoding=UTF8&psc=1&refRID=THXQCEEYTAE8D8QWRKXH

LimoStudio Photo Video Studio 10Ft Adjustable Muslin Background Backdrop Support System Stand, AGG1112
You can hang the green screen from this.
https://www.amazon.com/LimoStudio-Adjustable-Background-Backdrop-AGG1112/dp/B00E6GRHBO/ref=pd_bxgy_421_img_2?_encoding=UTF8&pd_rd_i=B00E6GRHBO&pd_rd_r=X80TTG9S2QN15HWD9HF8&pd_rd_w=VQddS&pd_rd_wg=UFkFL&psc=1&refRID=X80TTG9S2QN15HWD9HF8

Fancierstudio Chromakey Green Chromakey Blue Collapsible Backdrop Collapsible Reversible Background 5'x7' Chroma-Key Blue/Green by Fancierstudio RE2010 BG
This screen is very good if you want to show people sitting or standing if you do not show the ground.
https://www.amazon.com/dp/B00JSAOGWG?psc=1

Fovitec StudioPRO - 1x 7'6" Pop Out Muslin Backdrop & Reflector Clip Stand - [Includes Light Stand and Clip]
This is the stand that you probably also want to buy.
https://www.amazon.com/Fovitec-StudioPRO-Reflector-Backgrounds-Separately/dp/B00PLEX7Q4/ref=pd_bxgy_421_img_2?_encoding=UTF8&pd_rd_i=B00PLEX7Q4&pd_rd_r=YY9SB43FXFXG1KDN09HZ&pd_rd_w=f9pz8&pd_rd_wg=b75LN&psc=1&refRID=YY9SB43FXFXG1KDN09HZ

Lights

Having professional looking lighting will impress people that observe the change you made in the library.

Westcott Illusions uLite 2-Light Green Screen Photo Lighting Kit
You can buy good lighting to help enhance the picture quality when taking photos or recording in front of a green screen.
https://www.bhphotovideo.com/bnh/controller/home?O=&sku=904343&gclid=CjwKEAjwlKLHBRDztKr6wMnRthMSJAALcT-stnt-vFCEnQ0YbsWBQLOGU48LfLLjoHK8_q7TuitozxoCVZnw_wcB&Q=&ap=y&m=Y&c3api=1876%2C%7Bcreative%7D%2C%7Bkeyword%7D&is=REG&A=details

334

Green Screen Suit

LimoStudio Photo Video Chromakey Green Suit Green Chroma Key Body Suit for Photo Video Effect, AGG779 They make full body green screen suits. LimoStudio makes a highly rated product at a fair price. It is a safe choice. There are a number of companies that make full-body green screen suits. It is a good idea to shop around and read reviews. https://www.amazon.com/LimoStudio-Chromakey-Chroma-Effect-AGG779/dp/B005FMOX9M/ref=sr_1_1?ie=UTF8&qid=1492804332&sr=8-1&keywords=Green+Screen+Suit

Section 5 Screen Recorders

Screencastify - Screen Video Recorder Honorable Mention
You can record your computer screen with this extension.
https://chrome.google.com/webstore/detail/screencastify-screen-vide/mmeijimgabbpbgpdklnllpncmdofkcpn?hl=en

Flashback Express
This is a simple but very good free program to record your screen. This is a great place to start if you want to do screen recording with your class.
https://www.flashbackrecorder.com/express/

Loom - Video Recorder
This extension records your computer screen, and it also gets awesome reviews.
https://chrome.google.com/webstore/detail/loom-video-recorder-scree/liecbddmkiiihnedobmlmillhodjkdmb

Screen Recording for IOS 11
IOS 11 has a screen recording feature that can be turned on. This is good news for educators that want to record something on an iPad, Mac, or iPhone. It might be a problem for someone sending questionable images or text in social media.
https://9to5mac.com/2017/06/08/how-to-enable-screen-recording-ios-11-without-a-computer/

Screen cast-o-mac
You can record a video of your computer screen with this website.
https://screencast-o-matic.com

Windows Steps Recorder Hidden Gem
Windows has a secret hidden program called Steps
Recorder. This program records your steps with
screenshots. If you want to write directions, this program is
a way to make it happen much faster. Window 7, 8, and 10
have this program.
https://support.microsoft.com/en-us/help/22878/windows-
10-record-steps
https://www.lifewire.com/how-to-use-steps-recorder-
2626159

Section 6 HyperDocs

HyperDocs are not new. The concept of putting in links within a document is not new as well. Years ago, with webquests people were creating webpages for students using hyperlinks. What has changed is the quality of HyperDocs that are out there. People are combining HyperDocs with countless other technologies to create something awesome. Within HyperDocs, you can put links to other technologies, websites, videos, and pictures. Students get to add to your Hyperdocs as well. HyperDocs are often being created with Google Documents, but the concepts still hold true with Microsoft Word, webpages, or other programs that allow links and can be shared.

HyperDocs
This is a website about HyperDocs.
https://hyperdocs.co/

Teachers Give Teachers
This site allows teachers to share HyperDocs with each other.
https://www.hyperdocs.co/teachers_give_teachers

HyperDocs Templates
You can get some HyperDocs templates with this link.
https://hyperdocs.co/templates

HyperDocs Lessons
This Pinterest account has links to a number of webpages with HyperDocs.
https://www.pinterest.com/hiltoninptown/hyperdoc-digital-lesson-plans-~-hyperdocs/?lp=true

Section 7 Interactive Whiteboards

Websites

A Web Whiteboard
This is a very good interactive whiteboard that is online.
https://awwapp.com/

Twiddla
This is a very good and simple online whiteboard.
http://www.twiddla.com

Apps

Explain Everything EDU Honorable Mention
This is one of the most popular whiteboard apps around.
You can record a lesson with this app. You can even make
slides similar to a PowerPoint.
https://apps.apple.com/us/app/explain-edu/id431493086
Windows: https://www.microsoft.com/en-
us/store/apps/explain-everything-interactive-
whiteboard/9nblggh5gcw8
Google   Play:
https://play.google.com/store/apps/details?id=com.explaine
verything.explaineverything
Chrome:
https://chrome.google.com/webstore/detail/explain-
everything-whiteb/abgfnbfplmdnhfnonljpllnfcobfebag
Explain Everything Interactive Whiteboard
https://itunes.apple.com/us/app/explain-everything-
interactive-whiteboard/id1020339980?mt=8
Website: http://www.explaineverything.com/

https://whiteboard.explaineverything.com/

Educreations
This is one of the most popular free whiteboard apps. The app has a simple user interface and is a good whiteboard app. You can record lessons then share the lessons with students via the web. If you see the videos that teachers have created on the Educreations website, you will have better ideas of how why this app is popular.
https://www.educreations.com/
https://itunes.apple.com/us/app/educreations-interactive-whiteboard/id478617061?mt=8

Vittle
This is an app that allows you to annotate your pictures and PDFs. You can add audio and turn your presentations into cool videos.
https://itunes.apple.com/us/app/vittle/id629037418?mt=8
Website: http://www.qrayon.com/home/vittle/

LiveBoard Interactive Whiteboard
This is a whiteboard app that helps people collaborate on a task.
https://play.google.com/store/apps/details?id=com.inconceptlabs.liveboard

Whiteboard
This is a simple but effective whiteboard app.
https://play.google.com/store/apps/details?id=com.vistrav.whiteboard&hl=en

Software

OpenBoard
This is free whiteboard software for Windows or Mac computers.
http://openboard.ch/download.en.html

Section 8 Virtual Reality

Virtual reality and augmented reality are two amazing technologies. Those are valid reasons to include both in this book. Both technologies increase engagement. I believe that virtual reality technologies will be used with autism to teach social skills, emotions, and general human behavior. This is a safe environment for an individual to correct, improve, or develop social skills without the risks involved. I just believe most of the finer points of this technology has not been developed yet. Over time I expect motivated individuals to refine and more effectively use this technology for the purpose of helping individuals with autism. The amount of enthusiasm already generated in this area leads me to believe that this technology will develop for the next decade and beyond. If you have autism in your family or if you understand the challenges that parents, siblings, and teachers face you will also understand what is at stake. Technologist and speech and language pathologist have to unite to better lives with this awesome technology.

Virtual Reality Websites

Expeditions Best of Class
This is Google's virtual reality app. You can explore the universe from your classroom with this app. If you want to try virtual reality, this app is one you should explore.
https://edu.google.com/expeditions/
https://play.google.com/store/apps/details?id=com.google.vr.expeditions&hl=en
https://itunes.apple.com/us/app/expeditions/id1131711060

Google Cardboard
This is a virtual reality app that Google makes that can be used on your phone.
https://vr.google.com/cardboard/
https://play.google.com/store/apps/details?id=com.google.samples.apps.cardboarddemo&hl=en
https://itunes.apple.com/app/id987962261

CoSpaces – Make your own VR and AR Honorable Mention
The ratings on this app are okay, but the concept of making your own virtual reality is just that awesome. I see in the future people making their own virtual reality videos so that you can get the feel of attending an event that you can't attend.
https://cospaces.io/edu/
https://play.google.com/store/apps/details?id=delightex.cospaces
https://itunes.apple.com/us/app/cospaces-virtual-reality-for/id1091239872?ls=1&mt=8

Merge Cube Honorable Mention
This is augmented reality. You look at a cube with a smartphone, and it shows you all of these amazing visuals. There is more than one app associated with the Merge.
https://mergevr.com/educators
https://apps.apple.com/us/app/merge-explorer/id1453098606
https://apps.apple.com/us/app/galactic-explorer-merge-cube/id1253085468
https://apps.apple.com/us/app/mr-body-for-merge-cube/id1253085120

YouTube Honorable Mention

If you go on YouTube and search for virtual reality, you will find a ton of short videos. If you have a virtual reality headset, you can see a ton of amazing videos that work with headsets. The same videos work with a regular computer but are not as dynamic. You can find 360, 180, and 4K videos. The quality can vary. However, the videos, in general, are amazing. If you have a higher-end headset, it is like having an Imax movie theater in your head.
https://www.youtube.com/

You Visit

This is a virtual reality college touring website. You can watch the videos on a regular computer. However, with a virtual reality headset, you can get a much better experience. It is always a good idea to talk about college at an early age with students. This is a great way to show a student several colleges without taking a long, costly trip.
https://www.youvisit.com/collegesearch/

Catchy Words AR

You can teach young students words with this virtual reality app. You catch letters and construct a word. This app gets good reviews.
https://apps.apple.com/us/app/id1266039244
https://appadvice.com/game/app/catchy-words-ar/1266039244

Moatboat

This is a great idea for story creation. You type or say something, and it appears. If a student has writer's block, this would be a great tool to start the creativity.
http://www.moatboat.com/
https://apps.apple.com/us/app/moatboat/id1294845531

Nearpod VR Apps

Nearpod has a number of very good virtual reality videos. Nearpod is a reasonably priced service. If you want to get started with virtual reality quickly with quality products, then this is a viable option.

https://nearpod.com/s/science/8th-grade/types-of-alternative-energy-L32825263

https://nearpod.com/s/math/2nd-grade/fibonacci-in-nature-L32815133

https://nearpod.com/s/math/9th-grade/the-eiffel-tower-L32825741

https://nearpod.com/s/social-studies/9th-grade/the-boston-tea-party-L32816433

https://nearpod.com/s/social-studies/8th-grade/the-maya-L32823544

Discovery VR

Discovery has a number of virtual reality videos and an app as well.

https://www.youtube.com/playlist?list=PLiCk2I6PXl5qm0CTvO6zXt3k33GTmcIvk

http://www.discoveryvr.com/

https://itunes.apple.com/us/app/discovery-vr/id1030815031?mt=8

https://play.google.com/store/apps/details?id=com.discovery.DiscoveryVR&hl=en

Google Play Virtual Reality

Apollo 15 Moon Landing VR
You get a chance to see what it is like to walk on the moon with this app.
https://play.google.com/store/apps/details?id=com.Thomas
Kole.Apollo15VR

Titans of Space Cardboard VR
This is a brief tour of space with some in-app purchases.
https://play.google.com/store/apps/details?id=com.drashvr.t
itansofspacecb

VR Solar System
You get to explore the planets with this virtual reality app.
https://play.google.com/store/apps/details?id=com.onepixel
soft.solarsystemcb&hl=en

Mars Is A Real Place Cardboard
You get to see the surface of Mars with this app.
https://play.google.com/store/apps/details?id=com.drashvr.
marsisarealplacecb

VR Google Earth
You thought Google Earth was cool then try this. You get to see the earth in virtual reality.
https://vr.google.com/earth/

Mars Explorer
Mars is one of the most interesting planets. With this app, you get to explore Mars with this highly rated app.
https://play.google.com/store/apps/details?id=io.github.krtk
ush.marsexplorer

Bacteria VR 3D
You get to see what bacteria looks like up close with this app.
https://play.google.com/store/apps/details?id=com.renderne
t.bacteria&hl=en
https://itunes.apple.com/us/app/bacteria-
3d/id1168927717?mt=8

Human body (male) VR 3D
You get to explore the human body with this app. In this case, the example you get to see is the male body.
https://play.google.com/store/apps/details?id=com.renderne
t.humanmale&hl=en
.

The mechanism of hearing VR
This is a virtual tour of the human ear.
https://play.google.com/store/apps/details?id=com.renderne
t.hearing&hl=en

mozaWeb 3D Viewer
This company makes interactive books and virtual tours. The app allows you to play a number of dynamic animations. The app also gets very good reviews.
https://play.google.com/store/apps/details?id=com.renderne
t.mozaik3dviewer&hl=en
http://www.mozaweb.com/

Acropolis VR 3D
Take a virtual reality tour of the Acropolis with this app.
https://play.google.com/store/apps/details?id=com.renderne
t.acropolis&hl=en
https://itunes.apple.com/us/app/acropolis-interactive-
3d/id1001041071?mt=8

mozaWeb 3D Viewer
With this app, you can watch 3D videos.
https://play.google.com/store/apps/details?id=com.renderne
t.mozaik3dviewer&hl=en
https://itunes.apple.com/us/app/mozaweb-3d-
viewer/id1064850237?mt=8
https://play.google.com/store/apps/details?id=com.eonrealit
y.kingtutvr

360 Cities
This website shows you a number of cities via virtual reality.
https://www.360cities.net/

ZSpace
This company makes glasses that makes virtual reality come to life.
http://zspace.com/

Headsets for Virtual Reality

Mirage Solo with Daydream
I use this product. When I watch a video on YouTube, the quality is amazing.
https://www.lenovo.com/us/en/virtual-reality-and-smart-
devices/virtual-and-augmented-reality/lenovo-mirage-
solo/Mirage-Solo/p/ZZIRZRHVR01

Oculus
These are very popular virtual reality headsets. There is more than one to choose from. This brand also has gaming headsets.
https://www.oculus.com/?locale=en_US

iPads Apps

JigSpace
You can create and share three-dimensional images. The value of the app is best understood if you see the pictures of examples. If you are teaching with a diagram, this app will take you to the next level.
https://jig.space/
https://itunes.apple.com/us/app/jigspace/id1111193492?mt=8

Human Anatomy Atlas 2018
If you want to look at the human body up close without seeing the real thing, then this is it. The app gets good ratings with realistic pictures.
https://itunes.apple.com/us/app/human-anatomy-atlas-2018/id1117998129?mt=8

Section 9 Publishing

Being able to publish a book is a powerful tool. I remember my second-grade teacher had me publish a booklet. I was beyond struggling in school, but I remember that assignment because I wrote my first book. Hands-on lessons with a finished product help increase engagement. Students have multiple ways to present a story with added features. You can add pictures, an interesting design, and words. Some of the publishing apps allow dynamic videos. Everyone loves taking home a book for Mom.

Storybird.com
This website lets you upload pictures and create a children's book. A creative teacher could use this to create poetry or have students do a project. You can create a teacher account and classes. You make an online version of a book with pictures. Storybird.com will let you create an actual print book for money.
https://storybird.com

TikaTok
With this website, you can make a children's book. The concept makes writing in elementary school that much more fun.
https://www.tikatok.com/

Make Books with an iPad

Book Creator for iPad Author's Pick
You make a story, and you turn it into a PDF. You can insert pictures, video, and audio.
https://itunes.apple.com/us/app/book-creator-for-ipad/id442378070?mt=8
https://bookcreator.com/education/
https://bookcreator.com/education/resources/
https://app.bookcreator.com/

OverDrive Local Content

You can upload local content to OverDrive. If a school has OverDrive, you can publish your content onto your OverDrive account for anyone that has access to the website to check it out. All you have to do is convert your work to EPUB format and upload. Google Documents converts to EPUB format. You can also Google convert your current format to EPUB because there are many options. You can have your students enjoy being published. Of course, the content is only local, but we all have to start somewhere.
https://company.overdrive.com/2016/01/26/overdrive-local-content-lets-your-community-be-a-part-of-your-digital-collection/
Video:
https://cc.readytalk.com/cc/playback/Playback.do?id=3bt1f7
Convert Google Document to EPUB
https://www.techrepublic.com/article/how-to-export-your-google-doc-to-epub-and-give-readers-more-control/

Kid in Story Book Maker: Create and Share Personalized Photo Storybooks
This is a highly rated story making app.
https://itunes.apple.com/us/app/kid-in-story-book-maker-create/id594403164?mt=8

Kid in Story Book Maker: Create and Share Personalized Photo Storybooks
This is a highly rated storybook app for children.
https://itunes.apple.com/us/app/kid-in-story-book-maker-create-share-personalized-photo/id594403164?mt=8

Creative Book Builder
This book-making app allows you to make a book in HTML, EPUB, or PDF.
https://itunes.apple.com/us/app/id451041428?mt=8

My Story Book Creator School Edition
You can record your voice as well as self-publish a story. Then you can email the story. My Story has very good drawing tools that allow customization. You can take pictures to include in your story. This app is for young children.
http://itunes.apple.com/us/app/my-story-book-maker-for-kids/id449232368?mt=8

Word Processing Templates

Using templates are a free an easy way to create new projects for your students. You can create a newsletter, brochure, greeting card, poster, blog, website, or something else. There is something for most ages and subjects. When you expect students to write and add media, you increase the ways students can represent information and meet standards. You can allow your students to use different abilities and think on different levels. A picture is worth a thousand words, and a cool design can make a project something special. Of course, you can use these templates to represent materials to your students in more creative ways.

Google Templates Time Equitable
You can use these templates to do a number of projects. These templates can help you add creativity to your lessons.
https://docs.google.com/templates

Templates for Word Time Equitable
There are a number of free templates that come with MS Word. This can be very helpful if you are into project-oriented learning. You can create a poster, greeting card, brochure, newsletter, newspaper and any other template you can think of. Often times, you don't have to learn a new technology to do project-oriented learning. Using Word is a good example of doing project-oriented learning and not having to spend the time to learn a new technology. I also recommend using MS Publisher if your school has a copy.
https://templates.office.com/

iPACT
This app has templates based on the concept of Universal Design for Learning. The app gets good ratings and can be used to teach a number of different areas of education.
https://itunes.apple.com/us/app/ipact/id896725524?mt=8

Canva
There are a number of very good templates to help you design various visually appealing projects. A smart project-based learning classroom could do a lot with Canva.
https://www.canva.com/templates/reports/

Section 10 Curation Tools

In the modern world of teaching, there is a need or a want to share a number of electronic files. You can share websites, pictures, videos, or other electronic resources. This can mean a teacher is sharing electronic files or a group of students collaborating. The growth in this area is tremendous. File sharing is becoming the norm in many schools. Finding visually pleasing ways to organize a number of various files types is a powerful teaching tool.

Wakelet Best of Class
This is an amazing curation tool. You can share curated files with your students. The platform allows for collaboration and even integrates with Google Classroom and Google Suite.
https://wakelet.com
https://itunes.apple.com/us/app/wakelet/id1041331738?mt=8
https://play.google.com/store/apps/details?id=com.wakelet.wakelet&hl=en_US
https://chrome.google.com/webstore/detail/wakelet/iomokcfebnfiflpgcpcijfkfmafgkjgh?hl=en

Padlet

This is an excellent curation tool. If you want to share files, this is a great way to do so.

https://padlet.com/

https://itunes.apple.com/us/app/padlet/id834618886?ls=1&mt=8

https://play.google.com/store/apps/details?id=com.wallwisher.Padlet

https://chrome.google.com/webstore/detail/padlet/ppckapbnfhikdajgehibjapcohbaomhd?hl=en

Pinterest

This is a very powerful and popular online curation tool.

https://www.pinterest.com

https://play.google.com/store/apps/details?id=com.pinterest&_branch_match_id=651563201045497424

https://itunes.apple.com/us/app/pinterest/id429047995?mt=8

https://chrome.google.com/webstore/detail/pinterest-save-button/gpdjojdkbbmdfjfahjcgigfpmkopogic?hl=en

Chapter 11 Chrome

I made a section just for Chrome extensions because Chromebooks and the Chrome browser are so widely used. A massive number of schools have committed to Chrome products. As a result, many educators look for Chrome products first. With the number of options, people tend to look at what is on the platform that you use first.

Section 1 Text to Speech

Read Aloud: A Text to Speech Voice Reader Honorable
Mention
Read Aloud is very good at reading webpages.
https://chrome.google.com/webstore/detail/read-aloud-a-
text-to-spee/hdhinadidafjejdhmfkjgnolgimiaplp

Select and Speak - Text to Speech Honorable Mention
This text to speech app works with Google Documents.
https://chrome.google.com/webstore/detail/select-and-
speak-text-to/gfjopfpjmkcfgjpogepmdjmcnihfpokn

Talkie: FREE text-to-speech, many languages!
This is a text to speech extension that gets good reviews.
The extension also translates text into different languages.
https://chrome.google.com/webstore/detail/talkie-free-text-
to-speec/enfbcfmmdpdminapkflljhbfeejjhjjk

TTS Reader: Speech, Translation & Dictionary
This extension is designed to read articles, but you get so
much more. The extension will translate and act as a
dictionary. The technology is from Google. You can test
the extension for free, and it is very cheap to buy for a year.
The rating for this product is very good compared to this
class of technology.
https://chrome.google.com/webstore/detail/tts-reader-
speech-
transla/beofjdkoeblbffhccncmhnmbdngodmnm?hl=en

Voice Instead

If you want a more natural sounding voice and you are willing to pay a small fee for per year this is a good option. The is extension get good reviews.

https://chrome.google.com/webstore/detail/voice-instead/kphdioekpiaekpmlkhpaicehepbkccbf

Talking Web

This extension will read a webpage, or you can download it as a sound file. (.wave) You can even adjust the speed, voice, and language.

https://chrome.google.com/webstore/detail/talking-web/hdeikpphnbclpacdjdjjkpmbcacopnog?hl=en

ClaroSpeak

This text to speech extension has many good features to choose from.

https://chrome.google.com/webstore/detail/clarospeak/fblbeibikalffoohjpiojmpmmndpkeii?authuser=1

Speakit!

This is a Chrome app that reads what you highlight on your screen. I have tried it, and it works. The app works in the Chrome browser.

https://chrome.google.com/webstore/detail/speakit/ohpcoflekopkahpgomnabhkclbedepll?authuser=1

ChromeVox

This Chrome app reads the words on your screen. If you want to have the website read to you, this is a good app because it works. The app works in the Chrome browser.

http://www.chromevox.com/

Texthelp PDF Reader
This is a very good screen reader with a number of other tools to enhance the experience. The product is made by TextHelp. You can try it for 30 days, https://chrome.google.com/webstore/detail/texthelp-pdf-reader/feepmdlmhplaojabeoecaobfmibooaid?hl=en-GB

Snap&Read Universal
This is a text reader with OCR capability. You can try for free. The extension is made by TextHelp. https://chrome.google.com/webstore/detail/snapread-universal/mloajfnmjckfjbeeofcdaecbelnblden?hl=en

Section 2 OCR

Convertio
This extension converts from one file format to a different file format. If you look at the company's website, it converts a ton of file formats and works with a number of major cloud services. This technology comes in very handy when you are organizing electronic documents, or you need to convert to the right format for a text reader. The extension gets excellent reviews.
https://chrome.google.com/webstore/detail/convertio/eppjk efeiehhflmgkhdooajgbkkegpcl?hl=en
Convertiohttps://convertio.co/

OCR Converter - OCR Software
This extension will convert a picture, video, or PDF to text and then translate it into a number of languages.
https://chrome.google.com/webstore/detail/ocr-converter-ocr-softwar/npkagmamhfklkdmnhdimbmdgplpichdh?hl=en

Copyfish Free OCR Software
This extension will copy text from video, pictures, or PDF for various uses.
https://chrome.google.com/webstore/detail/copyfish-%F0%9F%90%9F-free-ocr-soft/eenjdnjldapjajjofmldgmkjaienebbj?hl=en

Project Naptha
This is an OCR reading app.
https://chrome.google.com/webstore/detail/project-naptha/molncoemjfmpgdkbdlbjmhlcgniigdnf

Section 3 Speech to Text

Voice To Text Notes App
This speech to text Chrome extension gets some great reviews.
https://chrome.google.com/webstore/detail/voice-to-text-notes-app/gmhndndomhenakopchancencmdeblnda

Speechnotes - Speech To Text Notepad
This is a note-taking app that has speech to text. The app gets outstanding reviews and is very easy to use.
https://chrome.google.com/webstore/detail/speechnotes-speech-to-tex/opekipbefdbacebgkjjdgoiofdbhocok

VoiceNote II - Speech to text
You type notes by talking to your computer with this Chrome app.
https://chrome.google.com/webstore/detail/voicenote-ii-speech-to-te/jimdfkeocobeeldobhpakapbhdeample?hl=en

VoiceIn Voice Typing
This speech to text extension works with numerous websites and gets good ratings.
https://chrome.google.com/webstore/detail/voicein-voice-typing/pjnefijmagpdjfhhkpljicbbpicelgko?hl=en

Online speech recognition - Speech Pad
This extension uses speech to text to help you search a website.
https://chrome.google.com/webstore/detail/online-speech-recognition/pehlbpmpoabkgenppepoaihkacolpdcf?hl=en

Voice to text notebook
This extension is a notepad with speech to text capability.
https://chrome.google.com/webstore/detail/voice-to-text-notebook/pjineiicgkijhommbbkldannmfmglbmf

Note Board
You can add pictures of videos and note-filled documents. The items are pinned like on a bulletin board.
https://chrome.google.com/webstore/detail/note-board/goficmpcgcnombioohjcgdhbaloknabb?utm_source=chrome-ntp-icon

Section 4 Special Education

ATbar
This free extension has some very valuable tools for accessibility.
https://chrome.google.com/webstore/detail/atbar/lihjlachbdi
cbhpalgegcgknkbmjhicl?hl=en

Task Timer
For elementary students, timers are a good way to set goals, create structure and expectations. For special education teachers and psychologist, this is a great way to keep pace with timed testing.
https://chrome.google.com/webstore/detail/task-
timer/aomfjmibjhhfdenfkpaodhnlhkolngif?hl=en-US

Premier Chrome Toolbar
This is an accessibility toolbar. This extension gets some good reviews.
https://chrome.google.com/webstore/detail/premier-
chrome-toolbar/aplnccdcmphhefocfbanabnifgcifpdd?hl=en

Worksheet Wizard
It will read the PDF to you. The extension allows you to annotate a PDF.
https://chrome.google.com/webstore/detail/worksheet-
wizard/pemjkjocagbbbpcpfalhelbaoelfgjhm?hl=en

Clicker Sentences
https://chrome.google.com/webstore/detail/clicker-
sentences/mjjoplcogfihnioljobfdpdcfplpcnbj?authuser=1
Website: http://www.cricksoft.com/us/products/chrome-
apps/clicker-chromebook-apps_home.aspx

Siteimprove Accessibility Checker
This tool checks the accessibility of a webpage.
https://chrome.google.com/webstore/detail/siteimprove-accessibility/efcfolpjihicnikpmhnmphjhhpiclljc?hl=en

Grackle Accessibility Checker for G Suite
This makes documents more accessible. Grackle checks the accessibility of the document and suggests changes.
https://chrome.google.com/webstore/detail/grackle-accessibility-che/copojmaamcpblldileiipebpfjahcnjf?hl=en
https://gsuite.google.com/marketplace/app/grackle_docs/1085622905455

Section 5 Reading

Bookshare Web Reader Honorable Mention
This reads Bookshare books with your Chrome browser.
https://chrome.google.com/webstore/detail/bookshare-web-reader/bkfmjmjngglphchhiemnghidpnddofmo

Learning Ally Link Honorable Mention
You can read books from Learning Ally with your Chrome browser.
https://chrome.google.com/webstore/detail/learning-ally-link/gdicnpbaekbefjanokchpfhnaphfnphl

Snap&Read Universal Honorable Mention
This app simplifies the webpage that you are reading, has optical character recognition, and reads to you. This is a popular accessibility extension.
https://chrome.google.com/webstore/detail/snapread-universal/mloajfnmjckfjbeeofcdaecbelnblden?hl=en

Newsela Honorable Mention
Newsela allows you to adjust the reading level to the student. You can have several students read the same article on different reading levels.
https://chrome.google.com/webstore/detail/newsela/bfpeiapdhnegnfcfkdfihabadngjagfj?utm_source=chrome-ntp-icon

Library Extension
This extension helps you access your local library as you visit different websites. This is a good way to save money for teachers and students that are looking for a number of books.
https://chrome.google.com/webstore/detail/library-extension/chkgcmmjoejpekoegkedcpifgfhpjmec?hl=en

BeeLine Reader

This puts a color gradient over what you read to make reading easier. The idea is different, but the good ratings are real.

Chrome:

https://chrome.google.com/webstore/detail/beeline-reader/ifjafammaookpiajfbedmacfldaiamgg?hl=en

OpenDyslexic Font for Chrome

This extension makes the webpage more readable by changing the fonts on the webpage that are easier on the eyes.

https://chrome.google.com/webstore/detail/opendyslexic-font-for-chr/cdnapgfjopgaggbmfgbiinmmbdcglnam?hl=en

EasyReader

This extension simplifies webpages to take away distractions.

https://chrome.google.com/webstore/detail/easyreader/boamfheepdiallipiieadpmnklbhadhc/

Mercury Reader

This extension gets rid of ads and distractions when you are trying to read online.

https://chrome.google.com/webstore/detail/mercury-reader/oknpjjbmpnndlpmnhmekjpocelpnlfdi

MagicScroll Web Reader

https://chrome.google.com/webstore/detail/magicscroll-web-reader/ecldhagehndokdmaiaigoaecbmbnmfkc

Booktrack Classroom

This is an interesting app. It plays a soundtrack to an eBook. It gets good ratings.

https://chrome.google.com/webstore/detail/booktrack-classroom/odmndfiaonleilpbajajkijoihjemocc?utm_source=chrome-ntp-icon

Section 6 Spelling/Grammar Checkers

Grammarly Best of Class Author's Pick
This free extension corrects your spelling and grammar.
The free version is very good. You can also buy a premium
version if you write all the time and need more. The
program also has a version that downloads to Microsoft
Word.
https://chrome.google.com/webstore/detail/grammarly-for-chrome/kbfnbcaeplbcioakkpcpgfkobkghlhen?hl=en
https://app.grammarly.com/

LanguageTool - Grammar Style Checker Honorable
Mention
This tool helps you make corrections. This extension gets
excellent reviews.
https://chrome.google.com/webstore/detail/languagetool-grammar-and/oldceeleldhonbafppcapldpdifcinji?hl=en

Spell checker and Grammar checker by Ginger Software
This app will help correct your spelling and grammar.
https://chrome.google.com/webstore/detail/spell-checker-and-grammar/kdfieneakcjfaiglcfcgkidlkmlijjnh?authuser=1

Grammar Checker
This is a grammar checker that gets some very good
reviews. It is not as well-known as some of the bigger
names but still a viable option. The company also has a
webpage that checks grammar. It is worth a look.
https://chrome.google.com/webstore/detail/grammar-checker/mpeepmfabickbdbckcejbflkpfamgcon?authuser=1
https://linangdata.com/grammar-checker/

GrammarBase - Web Grammar Checker
This Chrome extension checks grammar and gets some decent reviews.
https://chrome.google.com/webstore/detail/grammarbase-web-grammar-c/plklmneddckmpnnkjldofmaegchjmoea?authuser=1

Spell checker and Grammar checker
https://chrome.google.com/webstore/detail/spell-checker-and-grammar/dmgkiikdlhmpikkhpiplldicbnicmboc?authuser=1

Spellchecker.lu Mini
This extension will check your grammar and get some solid reviews.
https://chrome.google.com/webstore/detail/spellcheckerlu-mini/cmcmejmpjaeofdedldgfnpidfmnngdib?authuser=1

Learn 2 Spell
This extension helps teach spelling and vocabulary.
https://chrome.google.com/webstore/detail/learn-2-spell/bajhagkohgdkapnbflodncdgmpfhkolc?utm_source=chrome-ntp-icon

Section 7 Word Prediction

Read & Write (Chrome Extension) Best of Class
This Chrome extension has just about everything. Read & Write has word prediction that is excellent. The app has a picture dictionary. The extension has speech to text and text to speech. It does just about everything. The app creates a floating toolbar in the Chrome browser. This means a student can use Read & Write across all settings. It also means that a student can use Read & Write on any computer. That can eliminate the need for a laptop to travel with the student. It also means that a student could use this product at home with no extra cost or risk on the part of the school. The subscription is priced on the number of licenses purchased. The more licenses purchased, the less per license.
https://chrome.google.com/webstore/detail/readwrite-for-google-chro/inoeonmfapjbbkmdafoankkfajkcphgd
A teacher can get this extension for free. This allows teachers to test out the product.
https://www.texthelp.com/en-us/products/read-write/free-for-teachers/
https://gsuite.google.com/marketplace/app/readwrite_for_google_chrome/982754197589

These are extensions that are commonly used with Read & Write.
Snapverter
This web service works with Read & Write. Snapverter integrates with Google Drive. You upload a document to the Snapverter folder in Google Drive, and it converts the document to a format where the text can be read by Read & Write.
https://www.texthelp.com/en-us/products/snapverter/

Texthelp PDF Reader
This app will read and annotate PDFs. The app is often used with Read & Write from Texthelp.
https://chrome.google.com/webstore/detail/texthelp-pdf-reader/feepmdlmhplaojabeoecaobfmibooaid?hl=en-GB

Screenshot Reader
This extension reads selected content on a webpage. This extension can be used with Read & Write.
https://chrome.google.com/webstore/detail/screenshot-reader/enfolipbjmnmleonhhebhalojdpcpdoo?hl=en-US

Word Prediction

Word Q US 1 (Chrome)
This is a very good word prediction app.
https://chrome.google.com/webstore/detail/wordq-us-i/pojcommghdpcglmnodkpcdiknjfcgoge

Clicker Docs
You have to buy s a subscription.
https://chrome.google.com/webstore/detail/clicker-docs/glmkaoamkcjbpchpndkllpkonadidamf?authuser=1
Website: http://www.cricksoft.com/us/products/chrome-apps/clicker-chromebook-apps_home.aspx

Section 8 Memory

Quizlet Honorable Mention
This is the best flashcard website. You can study a number
of terms in several different ways. Quizlet has a massive
database of flashcards if you do not have time to make your
own on just about everything academic. The website even
has an assessment component.
https://chrome.google.com/webstore/detail/quizlet/bgofflge
ghkhocbociocnckocbjmomjh?hl=en

SnowLord's Quizlet Extension
This app works with Quizlet a flashcard website that
quizzes you with games.
https://chrome.google.com/webstore/detail/snowlords-
quizlet-extensi/ocpkldjgfaimjjemnlppehhgdbagajhp?hl=en

Vocabulary.com
This extension helps teach you vocabulary from
Vocabulary.com.
https://chrome.google.com/webstore/detail/vocabularycom/
nacjcabfneebdomlmehblfinaepipepd?hl=en-US

Wunderlist New Tab
Create a to-do list in a separate tab. This extension gets
very good reviews.
https://chrome.google.com/webstore/detail/wunderlist-new-
tab/fgikemaeelgbhjnhnnahcpkjpafaeion

Todoist: To-Do list and Task Manager
This is a very popular and highly rated to do list.
https://chrome.google.com/webstore/detail/todoist-to-do-
list-and-ta/jldhpllghnbhlbpcmnajkpdmadaolakh

373

Section 9 Assessment

Kahoot Smasher
The is an extension with good reviews for the very popular assessment website called Kahoot.
https://chrome.google.com/webstore/detail/kahoot-smasher/epbfmghopnodnekikikbfdaenmknpjdj?hl=en-US

Socrative Student
This is the student login for the very popular student response system.
https://chrome.google.com/webstore/detail/socrative-student/nblhpecglllndfihipmpdoikimcmgkha?hl=en

Socrative Teacher
This is the teacher login for Socrative.
https://chrome.google.com/webstore/detail/socrative-teacher/ofajgnplnindhnhnconjocimijjifaln?hl=en

Quizizz Student
This is an interactive way to quiz your class, and it integrates with Google Classroom.
https://chrome.google.com/webstore/detail/quizizz-student/iahpmdodigkpgbaolkdeelbflgeomhob?hl=en

GitHub Hovercard
This is a highly rated extension for the assessment service called GitHub. The extension gets outstanding reviews.
https://chrome.google.com/webstore/detail/github-hovercard/mmoahbbnojgkclgceahhakhnccimnplk?hl=en

Refined GitHub
This extension gets outstanding reviews. If you use GitHub, you should try this.
https://chrome.google.com/webstore/detail/refined-github/hlepfoohegkhhmjieoechaddaejaokhf?hl=en

Formative - G Suite Marketplace
This is an app for Chrome that works with the popular assessment tool.
https://gsuite.google.com/marketplace/app/formative/45549193519

Edulastic
If you use this assessment tool, this extension is a consideration.
https://chrome.google.com/webstore/detail/edulastic/mmmfookngjpgdahmnbbamplmbhleljio?hl=en
https://gsuite.google.com/marketplace/app/edulastic/1041286382143

Poll Everywhere for Google Slides
You can take a poll of all your students in real time. This is a great way to get feedback on your students.
https://chrome.google.com/webstore/detail/poll-everywhere-for-googl/jeehnidbmlhpkncbplipfalpjkhlokaa?utm_source=chrome-ntp-icon

Verso
This app helps you get feedback from your students.
https://chrome.google.com/webstore/detail/verso/plhfcehjadfjegljoflclmimcdbmnjpg?hl=en

ScootPad

This app teaches math and ELA and is linked to Common Core.

https://chrome.google.com/webstore/detail/scootpad/boihgp oojeingjbbdjmoocbdibophjap?hl=en

https://www.scootpad.com/index

Section 10 Notes

Diigo Web Collector - Capture and Annotate
This Chrome extension helps you to collect information from across the internet. You can save video and highlighted text. This is a great tool for collecting information for a report.
https://chrome.google.com/webstore/detail/diigo-web-collector-captu/pnhplgjpclknigjpccbcnmicgcieojbh?hl=en

Google Keep Chrome Extension
This is a very popular note-taking website product made by Google. This extension will make it faster and easier to access your Google Keep account.
https://chrome.google.com/webstore/detail/google-keep-chrome-extens/lpcaedmchfhocbbapmcbpinfpgnhiddi?utm_source=chrome-ntp-icon

OneNote Web Clipper
This allows you to save a ton of information on the internet to OneNote.
https://chrome.google.com/webstore/detail/onenote-web-clipper/gojbdfnpnhogfdgjbigejoaolejmgdhk?hl=en

Sticky Notes - Just popped up!
This is simple pop-up windows of notes.
https://chrome.google.com/webstore/detail/sticky-notes-just-popped/plpdjbappofmfbgdmhoaabefbobddchk?type=ext&hl=es-419

somnote

This is a very user-friendly and free notetaking extension.
https://chrome.google.com/webstore/detail/somnote/abfmic
iknijebdoghnlinglnifcobkkh?hl=en

Mic Note -Voice Recorder & Notepad

This is app will take notes and record what is being said at
the same time.
https://chrome.google.com/webstore/detail/mic-note-voice-
recorder-
n/nhkoenoennbjnibepkjdheodiaojdgpk?utm_source=chrom
e-app-launcher-search

Evernote Web Clipper

You can save webpages to your Evernote account with this
extension.
https://chrome.google.com/webstore/detail/evernote-web-
clipper/pioclpoplcdbaefihamjohnefbikjilc

Section 11 Annotations

Texthelp PDF Reader
This extension annotates webpages and reads to you. The annotation tools are quite good. This app can be used with Texthelp's Read & write.
https://chrome.google.com/webstore/detail/texthelp-pdf-reader/feepmdlmhplaojabeoecaobfmibooaid

Diigo
This is an organization and annotation tool. The website helps you keep bookmarks. You can also annotate PDFs.
https://chrome.google.com/webstore/detail/diigo-web-collector-captu/pnhplgjpclknigjpccbcnmicgcieojbh?hl=en

Kami - PDF and Document Annotation
This is an annotation tool. The extension works with Google Drive and Google Classroom.
https://chrome.google.com/webstore/detail/kami-pdf-and-document-ann/iljojpiodmlhoehoecppliohmplbgeij?hl=en
https://play.google.com/store/apps/details?id=com.diigo.android&hl=en
https://gsuite.google.com/marketplace/app/kami_pdf_and_document_markup/185741998891

Hypothesis - Web & PDF Annotation
You can annotate webpages and PDFs with this extension.
https://chrome.google.com/webstore/detail/hypothesis-web-pdf-annota/bjfhmglciegochdpefhhlphglcehbmek?hl=en

Kaizena

This website helps teachers give feedback to students.

Chrome: https://chrome.google.com/webstore/detail/kaizena-voice-comments/lhiccpgcnopcjjdobhoddnplkebplfaj

Website: https://kaizena.com/

Section 12 Citations

MyBib: Free Citation Generator Honorable Mention
This is an extension from a popular citation website. This app gets great reviews.
https://chrome.google.com/webstore/detail/mybib-free-citation-gener/phidhnmbkbkbkbknhldmpmnacgicphkf?hl=en

Apogee2 | Citation Creator
This extension will help you do your citations quickly.
https://chrome.google.com/webstore/detail/apogee2-citation-creator/gbbpnkefafembhibompejknmjndilgaj?hl=en

Cite This For Me: Web Citer
This app has one-click citations.
https://chrome.google.com/webstore/detail/cite-this-for-me-web-cite/nnnmhgkokpalnmbeighfomegjfkklkle?utm_source=chrome-ntp-icon

Section 13 Math

EquatIO Best of Class
This is a math editor that works with the Chrome browser. You can use a free version or pay for a premium version. Texthelp has made a number of outstanding products that can be accessed with Chrome. With so few good options for people with disabilities that are related to math this app I worth consideration.
https://chrome.google.com/webstore/detail/equatio-math-made-digital/hjngolefdpdnooamgdldlkjgmdcmcjnc
Website: https://www.texthelp.com/en-gb/company/education-blog/april-2017/math-made-digital-equatio-is-here/
https://www.microsoft.com/en-us/p/equatio/9p02xk38043p?activetab=pivot:overviewtab
https://m.equat.io/

Desmos Graphing Calculator Honorable Mention
This is a graphing calculator
This is a free graphing calculator website that is free and gets outstanding reviews.
https://www.desmos.com/calculator
https://play.google.com/store/apps/details?id=com.desmos.calculator&hl=en
https://itunes.apple.com/us/app/desmos-graphing-calculator/id653517540?mt=8
https://chrome.google.com/webstore/detail/desmos-graphing-calculato/bhdheahnajobgndecdbggfmcojekgdko?hl=en

GeoGebra Honorable Mention

This website has many graphing and geometry features. I recommend that you look at the website to understand the many features that are offered. You can use GeoGebra on all of the major platforms by download it or by using the website. There is a lot to like here. If you are a teacher or student that engages in the many activities on this platform. I recommend considering GeoGebra.

https://www.geogebra.org/
https://chrome.google.com/webstore/detail/geogebra-classic/bnbaboaihhkjoaolfnfoablhllahjnee?hl=en
https://itunes.apple.com/us/app/geogebra-graphing-calculator/id1146717204
https://www.microsoft.com/en-us/p/geogebra-classic/9wzdncrfj48n?activetab=pivot:overviewtab
https://play.google.com/store/apps/details?id=org.geogebra&hl=en_US

Graspable Math Sidebar

You can drag and drop equations from a webpage to this sidebar that the extension creates. You can enter in equations with an equation editor and rearrange equations that you drag from a webpage. This extension even integrates with Google Classroom. I recommend looking at their website. There are many features to read about. This extension is a hidden gem. There is a lot to like here.

https://graspablemath.com/learn
https://chrome.google.com/webstore/detail/graspable-math-sidebar/akhomcacccpndpgckgpkmcijkimphhmk?hl=en-US

Wikipedia with MathJax
This extension allows you to zoom into equations in Wikipedia. The app gets outstanding reviews.
https://chrome.google.com/webstore/detail/wikipedia-with-mathjax/fhomhkjcommffnlajeemenejemmegcmi?authuser=1

The Mathist - The Joy of Math
You can write your math notes better with this app.
https://chrome.google.com/webstore/detail/the-mathist-the-joy-of-ma/ehachmeohjhhbeehmhomikfanodljcnb?hl=en

IXL
IXL is a very popular online service that teaches math.
https://chrome.google.com/webstore/detail/ixl/ojpmknlmiefdmkfbfebehccibkjdihbj?hl=en-GB

Melanto Calculator Extension
This extension will add a calculator to the Chrome browser.
https://chrome.google.com/webstore/detail/melanto-calculator-extens/olhcajgllkpacioibcjiniefblpmpech?hl=en

Daum Equation Editor
People often do not think about typing math the way we do with written language. This is an equation editor for Chrome.
https://chrome.google.com/webstore/detail/daum-equation-editor/dinfmiceliiomokeofbocegmacmagjhe?hl=en

Algebra Calculator by MathPapa.com
This app goes beyond a classic calculator. It shows you all of the steps and helps teach you the process.
https://chrome.google.com/webstore/detail/algebra-calculator-by-mat/gdmnkbkgbigolamjjepkmicfhonpdfpi?hl=en

Math Games
This has a number of math games for preschool through 8th grade.
https://chrome.google.com/webstore/detail/math-games/ifaofecnoelaefbeocgnbfelcokffhan?hl=en

Section 14 Organization

Google Classroom Best of Class
When it comes to helping students with executive function issues, Google Classroom is a game changer. The fact that all of your assignments, papers, and information is in one spot helps all students. You can even hand in your assignments with Google Classroom.
https://classroom.google.com/ineligible
Google Classroom for Chrome:
https://chrome.google.com/webstore/detail/google-classroom/mfhehppjhmmnlfbbopchdfldgimhfhfk?hl=en

myHomework Student Planner Honorable Mention
Students can keep track of assignments with this.
https://chrome.google.com/webstore/detail/myhomework-student-planne/pembccdigcahnckbjcbehhcacplbbomj?hl=en

Doctopus
Doctopus helps you organize your Google Documents into folders. In the world of online folders, this becomes valuable. Doctopus is very helpful for teachers that want to organize student work into folders automatically. For teachers going paperless, this is a big step in the right direction.
https://chrome.google.com/webstore/detail/doctopus/ffhegaddkjpkfiemhhnphmnadfbkdhbf?hl=en

Mindomo - Mind Mapping and Concept
This is an outlining app for the Chrome browser.
https://chrome.google.com/webstore/detail/mindomo-mind-mapping-and/lomfkamlboaefcpcnnklebogoelalnjm

AwesomeDrive for Google Drive
This extension allows for one-click editing to Microsoft
Office products on Google Drive.
https://chrome.google.com/webstore/detail/awesomedrive-
for-google-d/aaebjepcfidgkojljbgoilgkgklehldj?hl=en

Flubaroo
This add-on helps you grade your students, give you useful
statistics, and it gets excellent ratings.
http://www.flubaroo.com/

Goobric Web App Launcher
This is a rubric creations tool add-on that is sometimes used
with Doctopus.
https://chrome.google.com/webstore/detail/goobric-web-
app-launcher/cepmakjlanepojocakadfpohnhhalfol?hl=en

Section 15 Presentations

Screencastify - Screen Video Recorder Honorable Mention
You can record the screen of your computer and even record yourself with a webcam.
https://chrome.google.com/webstore/detail/screencastify-screen-vide/mmeijimgabbpbgpdklnllpncmdofkcpn?utm_source=chrome-ntp-icon

Pear Deck Honorable Mention
This is an awesome presentation program that allows for feedback. This is a great way to present information and do an assessment.
https://chrome.google.com/webstore/detail/pear-deck/dnloadmamaeibnaadmfdfelflmmnbajd?utm_source=chrome-ntp-icon
https://gsuite.google.com/marketplace/app/formative/45549193519

PowToon Presentations Edu
This creates fun animations that can be used to create a presentation.
https://chrome.google.com/webstore/detail/powtoon-presentations-edu/ogodblbnhpbcmcjcoopbalconhnloagl?utm_source=chrome-ntp-icon

Haiku Deck
This is a popular presentation app. This is a good option for Chrome.
https://chrome.google.com/webstore/detail/haiku-deck/mipkilokfhepolbekmdghlclfnpfpief?utm_source=chrome-ntp-icon

Haiku Deck | Image & Template Search
This app has a ton of free templates to pick from. Haiku
Deck is a popular presentation program.
https://gsuite.google.com/marketplace/app/haiku_deck_ima
ge_template_search/153965991673

Storybird
Storybird creates interesting digital stories.
https://chrome.google.com/webstore/detail/storybird/khnklj
ecljfpgcoafnmoaanlhepgbfof?hl=en

Section 16 Writing

WriteWell Online Hidden Gem
The website is excellent. You can access a number of online templates from this website/Chrome extension. The Chrome extension has a number of templates to help organize writing and help with basic editing. This extension gets very good reviews as well. This is a hidden gem.
https://chrome.google.com/webstore/detail/writewell-online/obkdedbflcnbpillohfoghmjpekelpek?hl=en-US
https://writewellapp.com/

Book Creator
Book Creator is an outstanding platform to create a book with students within the classroom setting.
https://app.bookcreator.com/

MindMup
This is a very good outlining website/app.
Website: https://www.mindmup.com/
Old Version
Chrome: https://chrome.google.com/webstore/detail/mindmup-legacy-version/dnenaecjcgeppfpaokiifokeieopppej
New Version
Chrome: https://chrome.google.com/webstore/detail/mindmup-20-free-mind-map/mkgkheknpfngchmoaognoilfanomldfl

Writefull
This extension gives feedback to you on your writing.
https://chrome.google.com/webstore/detail/writefull/aolaabonkiegkggfdgjjehchjmjfanng

Draftback
This tracks your changes to a Google Document.
https://chrome.google.com/webstore/detail/draftback/nnajoi
emfpldioamchanognpjmocgkbg?utm_source=chrome-ntp-
icon

Quill
This app teaches grammar.
https://chrome.google.com/webstore/detail/quill/bponbohdn
bmecjheeeagoigamblomimg?hl=en

Google Dictionary (by Google)
You can get definitions of a word as you look at webpages.
https://chrome.google.com/webstore/detail/google-
dictionary-by-goog/mgijmajocgfcbeboacabfgobmjgjcoja

Power Thesaurus
If you are writing papers and want to expand your
vocabulary, then this is the app for you.
https://chrome.google.com/webstore/detail/power-
thesaurus/hhnjkanigjoiglnlopahbbjdbfhkndjk

Office Editing for Docs, Sheets & Slides
You can edit your Microsoft Office document with this
extension online.
https://chrome.google.com/webstore/detail/office-editing-
for-docs-s/gbkeegbaiigmenfmjfclcdgdpimamgkj?hl=en

Office Online
This is for Microsoft Office.
https://chrome.google.com/webstore/detail/office-
online/ndjpnladcallmjemlbaebfadecfhkepb?utm_source=ch
rome-ntp-icon

Google Dictionary (by Google)
You can get definitions of a word as you look at webpages.
https://chrome.google.com/webstore/detail/google-dictionary-by-goog/mgijmajocgfcbeboacabfgobmjgjcoja

Science Journal
This is a dynamic way to write your science journal. You can keep track of text, pictures, and recordings within this awesome app. The ratings are also good.
https://play.google.com/store/apps/details?id=com.google.android.apps.forscience.whistlepunk&hl=en&rdid=com.google.android.apps.forscience.whistlepunk

Comprehension Builder
This extension does a good job of teaching sentence structure.
https://chrome.google.com/webstore/detail/comprehension-builder/nlcglbnfhmmipbagabepebodfekpdifb?hl=en

Comprehension Builder 2
This extension teaches sentence structure. It is more advanced than the original.
https://chrome.google.com/webstore/detail/comprehension-builder-2/mipmnmjmmhclagalcbihemmfmiggeaei?hl=en

Section 17 Student Communication

Google Classroom Honorable Mention
This is one of the best tools to communicate and track student work.
https://classroom.google.com/ineligible
Google Classroom for Chrome:
 https://chrome.google.com/webstore/detail/google-classroom/mfhehppjhmmnlfbbopchdfldgimhfhfk?hl=en

Remind Honorable Mention
This allows you to send reminders to your class.
https://chrome.google.com/webstore/detail/remind/jppddpkfhdojffabldnpdacpeoefcljp?hl=en

Seesaw: The Learning Journal Honorable Mention
You can create a student portfolio with Seesaw.
https://chrome.google.com/webstore/detail/seesaw-the-learning-journ/adnohgfkodfphemhddnmikhflkolfjfh?hl=en

ClassDojo Extension Honorable Mention
This is a great program to keep track of students and communicate with parents.
https://chrome.google.com/webstore/detail/classdojo-extension/mbhcppckcncdempkomncfipbddlkofio?hl=en

Share to Classroom Honorable Mention
This extension is designed to have you share webpages to Google Classroom.
https://chrome.google.com/webstore/detail/share-to-classroom/adokjfanaflbkibffcbhihgihpgijcei?hl=en-US

TES Teach with Blendspace
This is an awesome lesson building website and app.
Website: https://www.tes.com/lessons?utm_source=chrome app&utm_content=v2
Chrome: https://chrome.google.com/webstore/detail/tes-teach-with-blendspace/agbdildaaolbagmahkbhgalikckjkjoi?utm_source=chrome-ntp-icon
iPad: https://itunes.apple.com/app/apple-store/id1124524449?mt=8

Edmodo
This is a very popular website/app that does many things. You can create teacher webpages and share links and tons of information.
https://chrome.google.com/webstore/detail/edmodo/ohpppancgeopfjndlaodikbinmkepfml?hl=en

Section 18 Whiteboards

Gynzy
This is a whiteboard app.
https://chrome.google.com/webstore/detail/gynzy/jhpccgpi
obbhpdafbjiflbfcdlklhkeh?hl=en

RealtimeBoard: Whiteboard for Collaboration
This is a whiteboard with a large number of features.
https://chrome.google.com/webstore/detail/realtimeboard-
whiteboard/opfmbdmhambgleempeofcjjhjclimccg

Ziteboard - zooming collaboration whiteboard
This whiteboard allows you to see what is being done in
"real-time." The whiteboard has a number of features.
https://chrome.google.com/webstore/detail/ziteboard-
zooming-
collabo/nldaeoadnnnkinljmmcabkgndhamjaji?hl=en

Explain Everything
You can get the classic whiteboard called Explain
Everything for Chrome, but it only works on Chrome OS.
https://chrome.google.com/webstore/detail/explain-
everything/abgfnbfplmdnhfnonljpllnfcobfebag?hl=en

Whiteboard Lite by Lesson Monkey
This is a very good whiteboard app.
https://chrome.google.com/webstore/detail/whiteboard-lite-
by-lesson/ncbecfmooieejbipmbjghhphmalleefe?hl=en

Section 19 Visually Impaired

Zoom for Google Chrome
This app allows you to zoom into a webpage.
https://chrome.google.com/webstore/detail/zoom-for-google-chrome/lajondecmobodlejlcjllhojikagldgd?hl=en

zoomWheel
This app allows you to enlarge a webpage.
https://chrome.google.com/webstore/detail/zoomwheel/kdfgigbjonaniokmpfflpflkhahhbaej?hl=en

Zoomy
This extension allows you to zoom into a webpage.
https://chrome.google.com/webstore/detail/zoomy/jgfonhdeiaaflpgphemdgfkjimojblie

Zoom on doubleclick
When you double click on an item on a webpage, you will zoom in on that object.
https://chrome.google.com/webstore/detail/zoom-on-doubleclick/jkmalmidnicnnmceielaelokkdmmgkcb?hl=en

Care your Eyes
With this app, you can change the colors on webpages to make it easier on your eyes to read.
https://chrome.google.com/webstore/detail/care-your-eyes/fidmpnedniahpnkeomejhnepmbdamlhl?hl=en

Screen Shader | Smart Screen Tinting
This extension takes away the hard light of the computer screen and gives you a softer light to read with. This extension is good for someone with older eyes or mild visual issues.
https://chrome.google.com/webstore/detail/screen-shader-flux-for-ch/fmlboobidmkelggdainpknloccojpppi?hl=en

Night Shift
You can change the colors of the browser for night time viewing of webpages.
https://chrome.google.com/webstore/detail/night-shift/fpnlpehjhijpamloppfjljenemeokfio?hl=en

Dark Reader
You can change your browser for night time viewing of webpages.
https://chrome.google.com/webstore/detail/dark-reader/eimadpbcbfnmbkopoojfekhnkhdbieeh?authuser=1

Manufactured by Amazon.ca
Bolton, ON

14145975R00219